ex libris
Nial Devitt

WILKIE COLLINS'S AMERICAN TOUR, 1873–4

The History of the Book

Series Editor: *Ann R. Hawkins*

Titles in this Series

Conservatism and the Quarterly Review: A Critical Analysis
Jonathan Cutmore (ed.)

Contributors to the Quarterly Review: A History, 1809–25
Jonathan Cutmore

Forthcoming Titles

Negotiated Knowledge: Medical Periodical Publishing in Scotland, 1733–1832
Fiona A. Macdonald

William Blake and the Art of Engraving
Mei-Ying Sung

www.pickeringchatto.com/historyofthebook

WILKIE COLLINS'S AMERICAN TOUR, 1873–4

BY

SUSAN R. HANES

MUNDUS INTELLECTUALIS

LONDON
PICKERING & CHATTO
2008

Published by Pickering & Chatto (Publishers) Limited
21 Bloomsbury Way, London WC1A 2TH

2252 Ridge Road, Brookfield, Vermont 05036-9704, USA

www.pickeringchatto.com

BRITISH LIBRARY CATALOGUING IN PUBLICATION DATA

Hanes, Susan R.
Wilkie Collins's American tour, 1873–4. – (The history of the book)
1. Collins, Wilkie, 1824–1889 – Appreciation – United States 2. Collins, Wilkie, 1824–1889 – Travel – United States 3. Collins, Wilkie, 1824–1889 – Oratory
I. Title

823.8

ISBN–13: 9781851969685

This publication is printed on acid-free paper that conforms to the American National Standard for the Permanence of Paper for Printed Library Materials.

Typeset by Pickering & Chatto (Publishers) Limited
Printed in the United Kingdom at the University Press, Cambridge

CONTENTS

In memory of
Samuel Houston Hanes
who first shared my dream with me

ACKNOWLEDGEMENTS

I wish to thank the curators and the staff of the institutions and libraries listed at the end of this book for making their holdings available to me. As a librarian myself, I especially recognize the exceptional cataloguing effort of manuscript librarians that has enabled me to locate rare Collins materials in unlikely places. Whether working in major libraries of the United States and Canada or in historical societies in small American towns, I was uniformly offered friendly and professional help. I thank Wendy Cowles Husser for her generous editorial assistance. To my fellow Wilkie Collins enthusiasts, Paul Lewis, Dr Andrew Gasson, and Dr William Baker of Northern Illinois University, I express my gratitude for their interest, encouragement and support. I would also like to recognize Faith Dawson Clarke and William Clarke, whose enthusiasm encouraged me and who have become treasured friends. Finally, I would like to recognize my husband, George Leonard. For his practical reasoning concerning Collins's travel schedules, his tireless assistance with the more trying aspects of primary archival research and his loving encouragement throughout this project, I am deeply grateful.

LIST OF FIGURES

Cabinet photograph of Wilkie Collins by New York photographer Napoleon Sarony (Author's collection).

PREFACE

> A kinder, warmer-hearted set of people surely does not exist, only their ways *are* queer.[1]

In the autumn of 1873, Victorian novelist Wilkie Collins began a six-month tour of America. Following the example of Charles Dickens and William Makepeace Thackeray, he arranged to give a series of public readings from his works, hoping he might achieve the same financial benefit that they had realized. He further hoped to promote his books, meet with friends and collect material for his writing. Unlike the earlier ventures of Dickens and Thackeray however, relatively little research has been devoted to Collins's American reading tour.

The intention of this study is to provide a sense of the America that Collins encountered and, in so doing, contribute to an understanding of the challenges and successes of celebrities who came to America in the second half of the nineteenth century. As a librarian, I have focused on providing a biographical narrative of Collins's tour, identifying where possible the 'stops' on his trip, and collecting the contemporary periodical reviews recording the reception of Collins's performances. As a result, this study provides the reader access to biographical and reception data not available outside of archives, but does not engage in a literary critical or literary theoretical discussion of those artefacts.

Study of the Dickens and Thackeray tours was significantly facilitated because both were accompanied by assistants who meticulously recorded their activities. Dickens travelled with George Dolby who carefully documented Dickens's time in America in *Dickens as I Knew Him*,[2] while Thackeray brought along Eyre Crowe who, as an artist and amanuensis, detailed their trip in *With Thackeray in America*.[3] Although Wilkie Collins hired his godson Frank Ward to assist him for part of his own tour, no records from Ward have been found. Published works about Collins's tour have been confined to short articles or chapters based on known letters, in spite of the fact that he gained impressions from his visit that would influence his writing for the remainder of his life.

Written almost seventy years ago, Clyde K. Hyder's article 'Wilkie Collins in America'[4] still contains the most comprehensive research on the topic. Hyder maintained that this period of Collins's life had been entirely neglected by biographers, and indeed, without his contribution, this observation might be true today. Citing newspaper reviews from New York, Boston, Chicago and Philadelphia, Hyder provided a sense of Collins's reception by the American press. He did not, however, investigate further the question of how Collins spent his six months on American soil.

Early biographies by Kenneth Robinson[5] and Nuel Pharr Davis,[6] published in the 1950s, offer little additional information about Collins's American tour. The fullest recent biographical accounts of Collins's travels to America are in *The King of Inventors: A Life of Wilkie Collins* by Catherine Peters[7] and *The Secret Life of Wilkie Collins* by William Clarke.[8] Peters, in her definitive biography, provides rich detail and brings together a vast amount of material. Collins's tour, however, comprises but a single twelve-page chapter. William Clarke, in his 2004 revision of *The Secret Life*, adds to the collected information about Collins's relationship with the Americans an account of Collins's meeting with theatrical producer Augustin Daly, but, again, confines the subject to one brief chapter.

Other recent publications relating to Wilkie Collins have added little to the collective knowledge of his American experience. In *Reality's Dark Light: The Sensational Wilkie Collins*,[9] Audrey Fisch perceptively focuses on *Armadale* (1866), *Black and White* (1869), *Miss or Mrs?* (1871), and *Guilty River* (1886), but makes no reference to Collins's experiences with and observations of postbellum America. Lyn Pykett's *Wilkie Collins*, part of the Oxford World Classics Authors in Context series, is a comprehensive study focusing on Collins's fiction from various perspectives, including historical, psychological, literary, and political. Pykett's discussion of race, however, relates primarily to *Armadale* and *The Moonstone* (1868), both of which were published before Collins's visit to America.[10] Lillian Nayder's *Wilkie Collins*,[11] part of Twayne's English Author Series, discusses Collins's works in historical context, but does not deal with his American experience. The *Cambridge Companion to Wilkie Collins*, edited by Jenny Bourne Taylor,[12] reflects new scholarship and places Collins's work within this critical framework. There is, however, no reference to his American tour.

In order to fill in the pages of Collins's American engagement book, I began with Clyde Hyder's article and with the two recently published collections of the Collins letters, *The Public Face of Wilkie Collins*[13] and *The Letters of Wilkie Collins*.[14] Using the dates and places provided by these sources, I consulted local newspapers for announcements and reviews of readings. When I found confirmation that an announced reading had actually taken place, I attempted to determine where Collins could logically have travelled next, taking into consideration the train schedules for the period 1873–4, the availability of suitable speaking venues, and the itinerary of Collins's friend and mentor, Charles Dickens. I then attempted to consult newspapers for such places during those times.

During my research, I visited over seventy-five academic and public libraries and historical societies throughout the eastern United States and Canada, and the Great Lakes area. I delved into special collections to look for unpublished notes, diaries, and letters, both by Collins and by those who might have come in contact with him. Although I felt it likely that Collins had spoken in Richmond, Virginia, in New Haven and Hartford, Connecticut, and in Erie, Pennsylvania, I was unable, despite significant effort, to find any evidence of such occurrences.

Eventually I was able to confirm 25 readings in 22 locations during the 154 days that Collins spent in North America. During his American tour, Collins used New York and Boston as bases from which he travelled to his readings. From these points of departure, he made short trips to nearby towns, including Philadelphia, and completed four major circuits, heading northwest to upstate New York, north to Canada, west to Chicago and south to Washington, DC. His first circuit encompassed Albany, Troy, Utica and Syracuse. His second was through Baltimore and Washington. His third was to Montreal, Toronto, Niagara and Buffalo and the final circuit was west to Cleveland, Sandusky, Toledo, Detroit and Chicago.

INTRODUCTION

During the second half of the nineteenth century, the lyceum movement in the United States began to evolve from its origins as a platform for education and self-improvement to a vehicle for public entertainment. In the movement's early stages, scientific lectures and debates, designed to 'educate and agitate', were the predominant subjects of lyceum programmes, but these gradually diminished as the American public clamoured for more entertaining pursuits.

There was no international copyright law to restrain the publication of popular fiction. American publishers habitually pirated the works of British authors, making them readily available to their readers. Thus the American public was well acquainted with the works of such popular writers as Dickens, Thackeray and Wilkie Collins and provided a ready audience for well-known authors who came to America.

In addition, improvements in transportation from the 1840s onwards enabled easier and more comfortable travel. Trans-Atlantic steamships made the trip to the United States feasible, and the expansion of the North American railroad system allowed for the possibility of one-night performances.[1]

In 1842, Charles Dickens made his first journey to the United States, receiving a hero's welcome. He dined with President John Tyler, attended sessions of Congress and was fêted everywhere he went. In spite of his open denigration of American customs and manners, and his criticism of international copyright issues, American readers flocked to see the charismatic author of the books they loved. They were not disappointed. Dickens's appeal led one reviewer to declare,

> He does not only *read* his story; he *acts* it. Each character ... is as completely assumed and individualized ... as though he was personating it in costume on the stage.[2]

After Dickens's first visit to the United States, Thackeray made his own journey. Thackeray saw that there was money to be made and determined that a lecture tour in America could provide an opportunity for financial security for his two daughters. He made two lecture tours in the 1850s: one in 1852–3 at the invitation of James T. Fields, and again in 1855–6 when he presented a series of lectures on the Hanoverian kings. The first tour was a personal and financial success, but the second was less so because of ill health and a negative press.[3] Nevertheless, he was able to carry home more than £9,500 from the two tours. In addition, he met with President Millard Fillmore and attended balls and other events in his honour. George Curtis summed up Thackeray's reception:

> Those who knew his books found the author in the lecturer. Those who did not know his books were charmed in the lecturer by what is charming in the author – the unaffected humanity, the tenderness, the sweetness, the genial play of fancy, and the sad touch of truth, with that glancing stroke of satire which, lightning-like, illumines while it withers.

Curtis continued:

> The lectures were even more delightful than the books, because the tone of the voice and the appearance of the man, the general personal magnetism, explained and alleviated so much that would otherwise have seemed doubtful or unfair.[4]

When Dickens returned to America in 1867–8 to conduct his own reading tour, Charles Eliot Norton wrote, 'No one thinks first of Mr. Dickens as a writer. He is at once, through his books, a friend'.[5] Indeed, hundreds of thousands of 'friends' had the opportunity to hear him read. In addition to earning the adulation of an entire continent, Dickens made a vast sum of money. Although he distrusted the American currency and insisted that the proceeds of his readings be converted to gold at a rate that cost him almost forty per cent, he netted almost £19,000.[6]

Taking inspiration from the successes of Dickens and Thackeray, many British celebrities undertook the challenge of an Atlantic crossing to seek the experience – and the fortune – promised by a tour in America. They returned home, eagerly sharing stories of what they had seen – and what they had earned.

By the 1850s, well-known American lecturers such as Ralph Waldo Emerson, Henry Ward Beecher and the abolitionist Wendell Phillips were not only inspiring their audiences, but also entertaining them with their impressive rhetoric. As the American public flocked to these programmes, promoters, operating through lecture bureaus, saw an opportunity for commercial success.[7] Lyceum tours became increasingly lucrative for both lecturer and promoter, and the bureaus actively pursued celebrities from both sides of the Atlantic. The bureau managers would make arrangements for an itinerary by scheduling productions, securing venues, and determining admission fees.

During the 1873 season that Wilkie Collins was in America, scores of English personalities were scheduled to lecture in the United States. They included Charles Bradlaugh, the notorious 'English Republican'; astronomer Richard Proctor; Gerald Massey, poet and Egyptologist; illusionist John Henry Pepper;

historian and traveller Hepworth Dixon and Mrs Scott Siddons, a Shakespearian orator.[8]

An editorial in the *Toronto Daily Globe* of that time explained the phenomenon:

> Since Mr. Dickens found his Golconda[9] in America, there has been an increasing tendency to bring every English celebrity, or even mere notorieties, across the Atlantic ... America is the paradise of the lecturer. Lecturing, an exotic in England, and but partially successful, is an indigenous plant in America, carefully cultivated and adequately remunerated. Therefore, any Englishman who thinks he has the power to interest an audience for a couple of hours, may very fairly take an opportunity of seeing the United States, and making money at the same time.[10]

1 FIRST CONSIDERATIONS OF AN AMERICAN TOUR

In a letter from Boston, dated 28 November 1867, Charles Dickens, in the course of his second American reading tour, wrote to his younger friend Wilkie Collins:

> The excitement in New York about the Readings being represented is quite unprecedented ... between ourselves, I have already some 2,000 pounds in hand before opening my lips ...[1]

On 3 December, he added:

> A most tremendous success last night. The whole city is perfectly mad about it today, and it is quite impossible that prospects could be more brilliant ...[2]

and again on 31 January 1868, from Philadelphia he wrote:

> We are getting now among smaller halls, but the audiences are immense. *Marigold* here last night (for the first time) bowled Philadelphia clean over.[3]

Such enthusiasm from his friend and mentor would not be lost on Collins as he shared vicariously in the resounding success of Dickens's second tour. The two men had grown close since their first collaboration in the amateur theatrical performance of Bulwer-Lytton's *Not So Bad as We Seem* in 1851. They had since co-authored such dramatic works as *The Frozen Deep* and *No Thoroughfare*, as well as working together on Dickens's weekly periodicals, *Household Words* and *All the Year Round*. The dream of a successful and lucrative run in America, as Dickens had achieved, might well have impressed the younger man and set him to considering the advantages of a reading tour of his own.

Collins's earliest writings revealed a fascination with the uncharted worlds of travel. His first novel, *Iolani*, was set in Tahiti and displayed 'a youthful imagination [run] riot among the noble savages', as Collins himself recalled.[4] Written as early as 1844, it was not published until 1991 when the manuscript emerged from private ownership. In 1850, *Antonina: or The Fall of Rome* was published.

Set in fifth-century Rome, the novel reveals Collins's attraction to the romantic aspect of foreign lands. In addition, he retained nostalgic memories of the trips that he made to the European continent with his parents as a young boy. It is hardly surprising that Collins would have been eager at the prospect of a journey to America.

By 1869, as the popularity of Collins's books continued to grow on both sides of the Atlantic, he was frequently writing to Harper & Brothers, his American publishers, about details of the publishing arrangements for his novels. He was also in contact with his Canadian publishers, Hunter, Rose, arranging for them to publish the novel *Man and Wife* in Canada in order to thwart frequent piracy of his American publications. A personal visit with his New World publishers would be a prudent business move.

On 6 September 1869, Collins wrote a letter to General John A. Dix, veteran of the American Civil War and, later, Governor of New York. Writing on behalf of his close friend Frederick Lehmann,[5] who was on his way to America, Collins alluded to a possible tour himself when he introduced his friend as 'the best representative I could possibly wish to have, until I am able to cross the Atlantic and speak for myself'.

In addition to Dix, Collins corresponded with a number of prominent Americans, including journalist and diplomat John Bigelow,[6] James T. Fields of the Boston publishers Ticknor & Fields[7] and George M. Towle,[8] a journalist who was on the staff of the *Boston Post.* Some ten years earlier, Collins had written to Lehmann, 'I have hundreds of American correspondents but no friends there'[9] but since that time, he had met numerous Americans visiting London and forged friendships though his associations with Dickens and others. These acquaintances might have led Collins to envision a visit where he would be welcomed and entertained by members of American society.

In a letter to American journalist C. S. Carter dated 27 February 1872, Collins declined the invitation to visit the US at that time, lamenting, 'There is no hope of my being able to make my appearance in the United States during the present year'. But, he added, 'I am seriously bent on doing all that I can to train myself successfully for a visit'.[10]

That Collins's plans to visit the US were well advanced was indicated in a review of a December 1872 lecture in New York by Edmund Yates, British novelist, dramatist and editor of the *World,* a London weekly:

> The lecture closed with a brief allusion to the traits of character of Wilkie Collins, but did not give a description of his personal appearance, for said he, 'I believe the author of *The Woman in White* contemplates visiting this country, and relating to you a story written on purpose for American audiences, in the course of a few months'.[11]

The three years between the time of Dickens's death in 1870 and the spring of 1873 were busy and productive ones for Collins. He published *Man and Wife* as a book, saw to the dramatic production of his novel *The Woman in White* at the Olympic, wrote *Poor Miss Finch* for *Cassell's Magazine,* penned *Miss or Mrs.?* for the *Graphic* magazine, wrote installments of *The New Magdalen* for the journal *Temple Bar,* published *Miss or Mrs.? and Other Stories* as a book, opened *Man and Wife* at the Prince of Wales, and published *The New Magdalen* as a book and also produced it as a play in Boston and London. In addition, both *The New Magdalen* and *The Woman in White* were due to be produced on Broadway. News of their success on the London stage peppered the *New York Times* 'Amusements' section in the spring of 1873.[12] A trip to America would allow him to be present for the New York premieres of both plays. Then, in the midst of these accomplishments, his only brother, Charley, died suddenly in April. Collins maintained nostalgic memories of the trips that he made to the Continent with his parents and Charley when they were young boys and it is likely that he would have considered going abroad as a way of dealing with his brother's untimely death.

Collins must have indicated the possibility of a visit to his US publishers, Harper & Brothers, because the 8 March 1873 issue of *Harper's Weekly* carried an ecstatic full-page article about Collins's background and achievements, including a giant engraving of the author:

> Mr. Collins has long cherished the intention of visiting this country, partly for the purpose of making an extended lecturing tour, and partly for the purpose of collecting materials for a new story, illustrative of life in the Western frontier. Ill health has prevented the accomplishment of this plan; but our readers will be glad to learn that rest and travel have so far restored his strength and he hopes to make the journey during the present year.[13]

On 10 March 1873, Collins wrote to his actor friend, Wybert Reeve:[14]

> I have had a great offer to go to America this autumn and 'read.' It would be very pleasant ... I am really thinking of the trip.[15]

Three days later in a letter to a Mrs Cunliffe[16] he stated:

> I have had a proposal to go there and 'read' which is all but irresistible to a poor man. If I <u>can</u> get away this autumn, I <u>must</u>.[17]

The following day, in a letter to publisher George Bentley,[18] he wrote:

> I have had a proposal for 'readings' this autumn addressed to me from New York, which deserves very serious consideration on my part.[19]

The proposal, disclosed in a 21 July 1873 letter to his solicitor, William F. Tindell, was from Charles S. Brelsford of the American Literary Bureau in New York.[20]

From the beginning, Collins had misgivings about Brelsford. In the same letter, he referred to him as 'the Speculator who offers to buy me for the US'. He wisely asked Tindell to thoroughly review the proposed letter of agreement. As he explained to Tindell, he would agree to give ten readings under Brelsford's auspices, after which he would 'be free to throw him over or to go on with him as experience decides me'. But realizing the importance of good relations with one's manager, he added,

> It is important not to say No too absolutely at starting as these people have all the machinery for managing the readings in their own hands and in excellent working order.[21]

Good management would be essential in such an undertaking, for it was reported in the *New York World* that Collins's agents had received over 1,500 applications for his appearances.[22]

As word began to spread in the United States of Collins's intended reading tour, announcements and snippets about him proliferated in the American newspapers. The *Boston Daily Globe* included his name in an article, 'The Coming Lecturers' on 26 March. The *New York Times* related the following anecdote in its 17 May edition:

> A Boston girl inquired at the library for 'Wilkes Calling Poor Bullfinch,' and when, after a while, she was given Wilkie Collins' 'Poor Miss Finch,' she went away satisfied.[23]

Although inaccurate, the *Baltimorean* included this announcement on 31 May 1873:

> Wilkie Collins will make his first appearance in August, at Boston, reading an original story. We would walk a mile or two to see the author of the *Woman in White*.[24]

In addition to requests for readings, Collins received invitations to make public appearances once he was in America, which he declined on general principle, sensing that the added stress of these engagements would have an adverse effect on his fragile constitution. In response to an invitation to appear before the Public School Teachers' Association, Collins tactfully wrote to the President, Joseph J. Casey on 12 July 1873,[25]

> Pray accept my thanks for your kind letter, and pray believe that I am gratefully sensible of the honor which the offered welcome of your Association confers on me. I feel the sincerest respect for the Public School Teachers of America. No other public duties, in any country, can compare in importance with the duties which the Teacher

> performs. The future of the nation is in his hands. But – while I feel sincerely proud of the recognition of my labors as a literary man which this greeting of your Association confers on me – there are reasons, I regret to say, that compel me to refrain from availing myself of the invitation which your letter conveys. I have (as you are perhaps aware) public engagements to fulfill on my arrival in the United States. My health is not good – and I am medically advised that I can only hope to contain the inevitable fatigue of the readings which I propose to give, by reserving all my energies for that one occupation, and by laying it down as a rule to abstain from appearing at public meetings.

Also in July, a representative of Harper & Brothers, evidently in response to correspondence from Collins, replied:

> We think you have acted wisely in deferring your trip to September. Our summer is very oppressive, the thermometer having reached during the last few days to 95 degrees in the shade, and this excessive heat is not unlikely to extend into the middle of September. But the American autumn, from about the 20th of September, is magnificent – and we hope that upon landing after a safe and pleasant voyage, you will be delighted, refreshed, and stimulated by our brilliant foliage, clear, bracing air and our brisk, busy life. We repeat the assurance that we shall be glad to contribute in every way in our power to the pleasure of your visit.[26]

As the summer of 1873 moved into autumn, Collins found himself 'worn out' by myriad obligations and responsibilities, both with his work and his private life. He complained to his Wall Street legal agent, William Booth, that after producing 'a Serial Story and two Plays in the last six months' he needed rest and a change of scene or he would never be fit for the voyage to the US in the autumn.[27]

Collins recognized that attempting to repeat Dickens's success in America required preparation and that he needed to gain experience in reading to an audience. He realized that reading aloud was not the same as putting a story on paper or acting a part on stage, although he certainly was experienced in both. In addition to novel writing, Collins had always been interested in theatrical pursuits. As early as 1838, he involved himself with amateur theatrical productions, writing, adapting, producing, and acting. In a production of *Raising the Wind*, Collins played the lead. He performed his part in Dickens's production of *Not So Bad as We Seem* before the Queen and subsequently travelled with the troupe when it performed before audiences of up to three thousand. It would seem that public readings would not be difficult for him to perfect.

An opportunity to read was first presented 28 June, when he read 'A Terribly Strange Bed' at a charity matinee at the Olympic theatre. Other items on the programme included actress Ada Cavendish reading 'The Charge of the Light Brigade' and religious composer Charles-François Gounod playing the piano.[28] Collins was not a hit. As Dickens's biographer Percy Fitzgerald observed,

> The impression he produced was that of all things in the world, he had selected the one for which he was least fitted.[29]

Actor Frank Archer was somewhat kinder about Collins's reading talents:

> He lacked the physique and varied gifts for a pubic reader, but what he did I thought was earnest and impressive.[30]

American reviews of Collins's London readings were contradictory. The *Atlanta Constitution* announced 'Wilkie Collins made his debut as a reader in London recently. The *Times* praises him very highly'.[31] The paper later added, 'His success was complete'.[32] But a review picked up by several American newspapers ran as follows:

> Wilkie Collins's first appearance as a reader in London recently was not a flattering success. His enunciation was indistinct, and his attempts to be funny and dramatic, after the matter of Dickens, were failures. He has a lucrative American engagement to fill and is working hard to acquire proficiency, but London people think it a little tough that he should practice upon them.[33]

Frank Leslie announced in his *Illustrated Newspaper*, 'Wilkie Collins is taking lessons in reading'.[34] The *Boston Daily Globe* reported on an early August reading and included the following quote from Collins:

> 'They [the readings] are but by which I, as an untried public reader, am endeavoring to train for my appearance elsewhere. I owe much to my American friends, and wish to do my very best to please them.'

The reviewer concluded that, although

> Mr. Wilkie Collins does not suit the action to the word so much as Mr. Dickens did, it is to be remembered that this is an accompaniment that grows with confidence and experience ...[35]

2 UNDERWAY TO AMERICA

Finally, the date was set for Collins's departure. On 18 July 1873, he wrote to William Tindell that he would be leaving for New York on 13 September and that, before departure, he felt it necessary to execute a new will for the security of his dependents. With Caroline Graves, his 'housekeeper' and her daughter Harriet, and with Martha Rudd (his morganatic[1] wife) and their two daughters, his responsibilities were many. Collins maintained these long-term relationships concurrently. Caroline and Harriet lived with Collins from about 1858 until his death in 1889. During a brief break in 1868 when Caroline left to marry someone else, Collins set up housekeeping with Martha Rudd, a woman more than twenty years his junior. Although the two never married, they assumed the name of Dawson and eventually had three children together. In addition, he was not in the best of health. He suffered from chronic 'rheumatic gout' and had been told he had a weak heart.[2] Two days before his departure, he signed a new will, leaving half of his estate to Caroline and Harriet for their lifetimes and the remainder to Martha and their children.[3]

The United States that Collins proposed to visit had a population of about forty million in 1873, spread across thirty-seven states and ten territories. The transcontinental railroad, completed in 1869, linked California with the east coast, and more than 60,000 miles of rail lines criss-crossed the country. As settlers sought new opportunities in the western territories, the United States Army continued to relentlessly pursue the Native American tribes; Custer's Last Stand was to occur three years later in 1876.

Following the end of the Civil War in 1865, the United States witnessed dramatic economic growth and the beginning of reconciliation between the Union North and the Confederate South. Railroad magnates, oilmen and financiers were amassing enormous wealth and the 'Gilded Age' was commencing. Greed and corruption riddled American politics, particularly during the administration of Ulysses S. Grant, the venerated Civil War general who was elected to his second term as President in November 1872.

The front pages of the newspapers were dominated by fears of war with Spain over issues with Cuba, the wreck of the British steamship *Atlantic* off the coast of Nova Scotia, fighting between Indians and settlers, and continuous reports of fires, explosions, robberies and murders.

Collins booked passage to America aboard the Cunard Line's *Algeria,* one of a trio of modern ships built in the late 1860s. Although the ship was state of the art, he was nonetheless aware of the hazards of ocean travel. Journeys across the Atlantic still held significant risk. According to a report in the *New York Times,* from 1840 to the end of 1873, 48 steamers crossing between New York and Europe had been lost,[4] a number significant enough to give any traveller second thoughts. In February 1873, the *Northfleet* had lost 343, and as recently as 31 March 1873 the British steamship *Atlantic,* of the White Star Line, travelling from Liverpool to New York, struck on Meagher's Rock, Nova Scotia, losing 546 of its 952 passengers.[5]

The ship sailed from Liverpool, with a stop at Queenstown, Ireland.[6] The crossing took twelve days and was apparently uneventful. But as Collins was steaming toward the American continent, a financial crisis of mammoth proportions was unfolding in major US markets. On 18 September, the Philadelphia banking firm of Jay Cooke – the banker who during the Civil War had made vast sums, in commissions alone, for selling government bonds – declared bankruptcy, precipitating a financial panic affecting not only New York City but the entire United States, as banks and trust companies failed. Five thousand businesses closed and put their workers on the street, leaving millions penniless and only the very rich secure.[7] The impact of this disaster was graphically described in a special supplement of *Frank Leslie's Illustrated Newspaper*: [8]

> The Great Financial Panic
> CRASH IN WALL STREET
> RUSH ON THE BANKS
>
> The financial crisis through which our country, but more especially New York City, is now passing, marks an era in our history that can never be forgotten. The ruin and failure wrought by this crash upon our money institutions is simply frightful to contemplate. Men who a few days ago were worth millions are today penniless. Banks and trust companies whose credit was considered as impregnable as the Government itself are today bankrupt.

As he crossed the Atlantic, Collins would have had no inkling of the effect of the panic on his audiences and on his financial success as a reader. Nor could he know how his managers would handle the panic in their arrangements for his performances.

On Thursday, 25 September, the *Algeria* steamed into New York harbour.[9] At the dock to meet him was his old friend, the actor Charles Fechter.[10] The two met when he was performing in London in 1860 and they later collaborated on *Black and White,* a play that Collins wrote in 1869. Later that year, Fechter left for the US where he bought a small farm near Philadelphia, Pennsylvania.

As Collins later recalled, 'Fechter's was the first face I saw on disembarking on the wharf'.[11] After exchanging greetings, the two went to the cosy Westminster Hotel at Irving Place where they both were to stay. Delegations from the exclusive Arcadian Club and Lotos Club were stationed at the hotel to greet the novelist[12] and welcome him to the city of 4.5 million people. After extricating himself from his well-wishers, Collins was shown to his rooms, the same suite, with a private door and staircase, that Dickens had occupied six years before. According to reports, the younger man was quite moved to see his mentor's desk.[13] Later that evening Fechter was on hand to help Collins order his first American dinner. Afterward, Collins recalled:

> He left me at night with a parting flash of the old gayety. 'You will find friends here, wherever you go,' he said; 'Don't forget that I was the friend who introduced you to Soft Shell Crab.'[14]

Actor Wybert Reeve was to have accompanied Collins on his Atlantic crossing. He was delayed, however, eventually arriving in Boston aboard the Cunard's *Parthia* on 15 November 1873.[15] He later wrote in his 'Recollections of Wilkie Collins' the extent to which Collins was hounded by reporters and interviewers during his first two or three weeks in America. He related an incident that greatly amused Collins shortly after his arrival in New York:

> Before leaving England [Collins] found himself in want of a rough traveling suit of clothes, and driving though [London] he turned into Moses' great emporium and bought a cheap shoddy suit. The *New York Herald*, in describing Collins, gave an elaborate account of his person. He was wearing at the time the slop suit, and the description wound up with the statement that Mr. Collins was evidently a connoisseur of dress. He had on one of those stylish West End tailor's suits of a fashionable cut by which an Englishman of taste is known.[16]

Speculation about Collins's actual reading schedule began as soon as he arrived on American shores. The *New York Herald* stated that it was 'the intention of Mr. Collins to give 100 readings in this country previous to his return home' and that 'the American Literary Bureau would manage the entertainments'. The article proceeded to optimistically announce that Collins would be reading

> in the larger cities and great towns of Western and Central New York, Pennsylvania, and others of the Middle and Western States, 'going West' as far as St. Louis. From thence Mr. Collins will progress to New England, visiting Boston, Providence, and other places, and will return to New York October 30. In New York he will give a series of six readings, probably in Steinway Hall ... It is also believed that Mr. Collins will visit the Pacific slope and the Yosemite Valley previous to his return.[17]

3 AN AUSPICIOUS WELCOME: NEW YORK CITY

Two days after his arrival, on a Saturday evening, Collins was honoured at a reception and dinner at the Lotos Club. Chartered in 1870, the Club's purpose was to 'promote social intercourse among journalists, literary men, artists and members of the music and dramatic professions, and such merchants and professional gentlemen of artistic tastes and inclinations as would naturally be attracted by such a club'.[1] Over the years, the Club had entertained such distinguished visitors as Charles Dickens and composer Jacques Offenbach.[2] The engraved invitation to the Dinner to Wilkie Collins indicated that the evening was to be held at the Club House at No. 2 Irving Place and would begin at 9.00 p.m.[3] Whitelaw Reid, President of the Lotos, would preside.

In attendance were 'many persons of distinction', including poets, novelists, editors, painters, operatic stars and actors.[4] Among the guests were author Bret Harte, Italian tragedian Tommaso Salvini and Charles Bradlaugh. Collins's US promoter, Charles S. Brelsford, a Lotos member, was also present; 'a scrawny, sickly Yankee, but a good fellow and capable manager' according to Lotos historian, John Elderkin.[5] Numerous newspaper accounts both at home and abroad covered an event that brought out the best and the brightest of American and European culture, albeit all male. As one newspaper described the evening, it was 'a stag affair, and cigar smoke replaced the perfumed air which indicates the presence of the sex'.[6]

Although it was reported that the evening started out 'thin' at 9.00, by 10.30 'every part of the club house was crowded'.[7] The guest of honour showed up at 11.00 and was welcomed by President Reid. He introduced Collins and spoke of him 'in the most gracious and flattering terms as a writer',[8] saying,

> We have met tonight to greet a visitor from the other side, of whom nothing is unknown to us but his face. May he give us long and frequent opportunity for better acquaintance with that. Thackeray once closed a charming paper on an American author with words which we may fitly take up and apply in turn to our English guest: 'It has been his fortunate lot to give great happiness and delight to the world, which thanks him in return with an immense kindliness, respect, affection'. [Applause.] And

as Thackeray's great companion in work and fame, our guest's name is a familiar association with his, in America, for we had come to prize him as the friend and literary associate of Charles Dickens even before we had learned to honor him yet more for his own sake.[9]

Collins then came forward and 'was received with great enthusiasm'.[10] He gave a speech in which he spoke of his experiences with American hospitality and the kindness that he had received from Americans.

MR. PRESIDENT AND GENTLEMEN: Many years ago – more years than I now quite like to reckon – I was visiting Sorrento, in the Bay of Naples, with my father, mother and brother, as a boy of thirteen. At that time of my life, as at this time of my life, I was an insatiable reader of that order of books for which heavy people have invented the name of 'light literature.' [Laughter.] In due course of time I exhausted the modest resources of the library which we had brought to Naples, and found myself faced with the necessity of borrowing from the resources of our fellow travelers, summer residents of Sorrento like ourselves. Among them was a certain countryman of yours, very tall, very lean, very silent, and very melancholy. Under what circumstances the melancholy of this gentleman took its rise I am not able to tell you. The ladies thought it was a disappointment in love; the men attributed it to a cause infinitely more serious than that – I mean indigestion. Whether he suffered in heart or whether he suffered in stomach, I took, I remember, a boy's unreasonable fancy to him, passing over dozens of other people, apparently far more acceptable than he was. I ventured to look up to the tall American – it was a long way to look up-and said in a trembling voice: 'Can you lend me a book to read?' He looked down to me – it was a long way to look down – and said I have got but two amusing books; one of them is 'The Sorrows of Werther', and the other is 'The Sentimental journey'. [Laughter.] 'You are heartily welcome to both these books. Take them home and when you have read them, bring them back and dine with me, and tell me what you think of them.' I took them home and read them, and told him what thought of them, much more freely than I would now, and last, not least, I had an excellent dinner crowned with a cake, which was an epoch in my youthful existence, and which, I may say, lives gratefully and greasily in my memory to the present day. [*Applause*] Now, Mr. President and gentlemen, I venture to tell you this for one reason. It marks my first experience with American kindness and American hospitality. In many different ways this early expression of your kindness and hospitality has mingled in my after-life, now in England, now on the Continent, until it has culminated in this magnificent reception from the Lotos Club. I am not only gratified but touched by the manner in which you have greeted me, and the cordiality with which the remarks of your President have been received. I venture to say that I see in this reception something more than a recognition of my humble labors only. I think I see a recognition of English literature, liberal, spontaneous and sincere, which I think is an honor to you as well as an honor to me. In the name of English literature, I beg gratefully to thank you. On my own behalf, I beg to assure you that I shall not soon forget the encouragement you have offered to me, at the outset of my career in America. Permit me to remind you that I am

> now speaking the language of sincere gratitude, and that is essentially a language of very few words.[11]

One newspaper account concluded, 'Before he had finished he had won the hearts of all present'.[12] The guests adjourned to the supper room for a large banquet, described in one report as 'an elegant collation'.[13] Numerous speeches were given, including words by poet John Saxe, Rev. Edwin H. Chapin and District Attorney B. K. Phelps. A toast was drunk to Collins's health 'amid prolonged cheering'. He answered with a single sentence of thanks. Signor Salvini, the Italian dramatist, responded to the toast in his honour with 'an exceedingly graceful little speech in Italian'.[14] Towards the end of the evening, there were calls for a speech from the Republican orator, Charles Bradlaugh, who

> thanked the Club for the opportunity to unite with them in testifying his regard and admiration for his distinguished fellow countryman, whom he met – since they belonged to different classes at home – for the first time on foreign soil. It was a privilege, he said, which no club in England would accord him.[15]

This appearance by the controversial freethinking and free-speaking Bradlaugh was not, however, universally condoned. In a sharply worded editorial entitled 'Bad Taste', the *Kingston Whig* questioned the judgment of the Lotos Club in even allowing 'the Atheist and Republican Bradlaugh' to be present, not to mention be met with cheers, at an evening honouring the respected novelist:

> Had they resolved to offer a direct insult to Mr. Collins, they could not have chosen a more effective mode than by ostentatiously parading their approval of such a man as Bradlaugh ... Mr. Collins, we are glad to say, let the Lotos Club's display of bad taste pass with a quiet sarcasm, but not the less will the Club suffer in reputation for its want of courtesy.[16]

A more thoughtful response to Bradlaugh's presence was noted in the *Commercial Advertiser*. After recording Bradlaugh's comments, the paper concluded:

> And indeed the sight [of those present] must have been an impressive one to the man of erratic theories. The picked men of all classes surrounded him – picked not because of the accident of birth or fortune, but for the success which each had achieved in his line of life. No war against riches, royalty, or religion could have evolved so true a democracy. Centuries ago, Euripides wrote: 'Time, as it grows old, teaches all things.' And Mr. Bradlaugh may learn from his experience of Saturday night that the grandest revolutions are those wrought out in silence, and committed to the fostering care of time.[17]

The evening proved an amazing introduction to Collins's American experience, and perhaps more illustrative of the collective American character than he could have imagined. Wybert Reeve, walking Collins back to the hotel, recalled, 'It was a delightful evening, ending, indeed, when morning was breaking'.[18]

The Rigours of New York City

As Collins wrote to Jane Bigelow, beautiful wife of American diplomat John Bigelow, a few days after the Lotos banquet, he was already finding 'himself living ... in a species of social whirlwind'.[19] He mentioned that he had been at the theatre the night before and was to dine with a group of men that evening. He was a frequent guest at the Lotos Club, particularly on Ladies' Nights, where he was reported to be 'so good natured and so small that ladies ask him all sorts of naïve questions'.[20] Harper & Brothers, in a letter to Charles Reade, noted, 'Wilkie Collins, whom we have seen repeatedly since his arrival in New York, seems to be enjoying his American sights and sensations'.[21]

In addition to the invitations and solicitations of friends and well- wishers, Collins was hounded by reporters. In her *Memories of Victorian London*, Lucy Walford recalled Collins's description of his experiences with the American press, especially women:

> They pursued me everywhere. One day I went to make a call at a quiet house, not at all a house where publicity is courted, and had hardly sat down when the door opened and in came a lady, little black bag in one hand and her card in the other. Could she have a few minutes' conversation; she was the representative of some paper or other, I forget which. It was too bad; I turned to my hostess to apologize for the impertinence, thinking she would resent it as I did, and she was actually laughing! And she implored me not to disappoint the poor, hungry lady. 'Remember, it is her daily bread,' she murmured in my ear.
>
> After that I made a determined effort to get my interviewers to come in batches, and one day went back to the hotel to find twelve feminine editors of journals large and small, seated in a circle, waiting for my return! They seemed to have formed a sort of alliance, for no sooner had I made my bow than the oldest and ugliest of them stood forth and solemnly observing, 'Let me embrace you for the company,' offered me a chaste salute.
>
> However much I might have appreciated the same from a youthful beauty, I did not exactly court a repetition of it thus bestowed, and next day there were very moderate praises of my personal charms in consequence. I suppose I did look grim, for I felt it. Really, they were not attractive –[22]

There was much to assimilate of the Americans and their strange ways. A contemporary tourist handbook, in a chapter providing 'General Hints', advised the traveller to

> reconcile himself to the absence of deference or servility on the part of those he considers his social inferiors; but if ready himself to be courteous on a footing of equality he will seldom meet any real impoliteness.[23]

This facet of American life was illustrated by an incident that Wybert Reeve later described. He and Collins witnessed the following scene when they were invited to dinner at a grand house on Fifth Avenue one Sunday evening:

> Arriving there, we were received by the host and hostess. They both seemed very uncomfortable, and I had noticed that a young lady opened the front door to us. At length the hostess asked us to excuse the want of servants and the dinner, which consisted of a piece of cold meat, some fruit and cheese. She explained that the servants objected to guests in the house on Sunday, as they wished to have the day to themselves. They had been humbly asked by their mistress to permit it on this occasion, and they graciously acknowledged they might have done so if they had had a week's notice to make their arrangements; but as it was the thing was quite out of the question, and accordingly they had walked out of the house.[24]

The handbook described other customs that Collins would discover for himself:

> The average Englishman will probably find the chief physical discomforts in the dirt of the city streets, the roughness of the country roads, the winter overheating in hotels and railway cars (70-75 degrees Fahrenheit being by no means unusual), and (in many places) the habit of spitting on the floor; but the Americans themselves are now keenly alive to these weak points and are doing their best to remove them.[25]

Another trait of Americans that Collins noted was their reluctance to enjoy physical exercise. He developed a daily habit of walking from Union Square to Central Park and back, a distance of about ten miles, but inevitably,

> Half a dozen times on my way, friends in carriages would stop and beg me to jump in. I always declined, and I really believe that they regarded my walking exploits as a piece of English eccentricity.[26]

On Wednesday, 1 October, John Bigelow called on Collins at his hotel. Collins was packing to join his friend Charles Fechter at his Pennsylvania farm. Although he had only been in New York a week, he was already overwhelmed. He confided to Bigelow that he had so many visitors that he had not a moment to himself. Although he had been inundated with attention, Bigelow commented in his journal that Collins was looking much better than when last he saw him, years earlier in London.[27]

Before he could escape to the quiet of eastern Pennsylvania, Collins was honoured at another dinner. That evening, Samuel S. Conant, editor of *Harper's Weekly,* hosted a banquet for Collins at the Century Club.[28] John Elderkin, historian of the rival Lotos Club described the Century as

> a most venerable and moss-grown institution ... a club, composed of authors, artists and amateurs, with inherited traditions, and the best and strongest men in the professions, and, therefore, naturally somewhat exclusive.[29]

The guest list[30] included some sixty or seventy writers, journalists, and artists. One attendee, John Parton, excitedly wrote to his stepdaughter Ellen 'this evening I dine with Wilkie Collins at the Century Club'. He had been unable to attend the Lotos banquet, a fact he noted on the engraved invitation he kept as a souvenir.[31] Unfortunately, the prominent poet, William Cullen Bryant, wrote that he would not be able to attend the function.[32]

The *New York World* reported, 'The repast was in the best style of the Century Club'.[33] The lengthy menu included oysters, followed by a soup course of bisque of crabs and consommé; boiled Spanish mackerel, fillet of beef with mushroom sauce, boiled turkey with celery sauce and roast ham with Champagne sauce; tomatoes Farcie, potato croquettes and cauliflower; sweetbreads with green peas, boiled chicken partridge and celery salad; Neufchatel cheese, ice cream, Charlotte Russe and fruits; coffee, liquors and Roman punch; and Russian cigarettes and cigars.[34] (Figure 3.1)

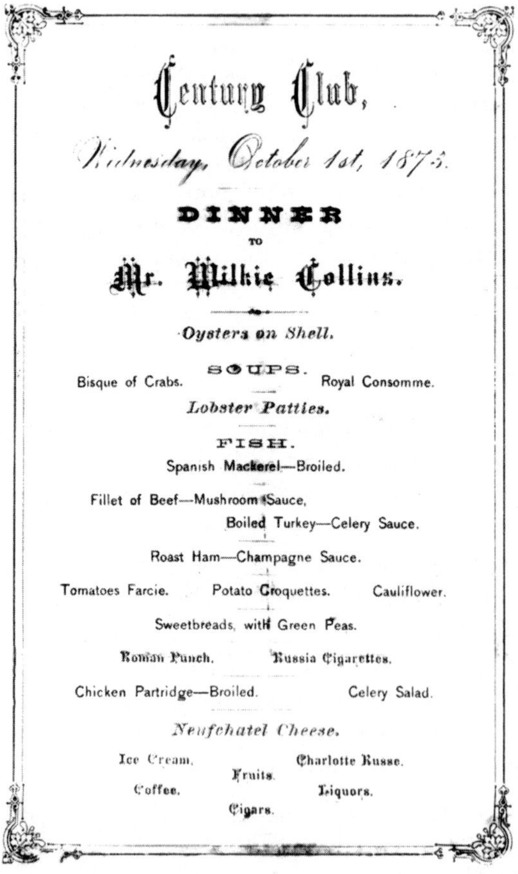
Century Club,
Wednesday, October 1st, 1873.
DINNER
TO
Mr. Wilkie Collins.
Oysters on Shell.
SOUPS.
Bisque of Crabs. Royal Consomme.
Lobster Patties.
FISH.
Spanish Mackerel—Broiled.
Fillet of Beef—Mushroom Sauce,
Boiled Turkey—Celery Sauce.
Roast Ham—Champagne Sauce.
Tomatoes Farcie. Potato Croquettes. Cauliflower.
Sweetbreads, with Green Peas.
Roman Punch. Russia Cigarettes.
Chicken Partridge—Broiled. Celery Salad.
Neufchatel Cheese.
Ice Cream. Charlotte Russe.
Fruits.
Coffee. Liquors.
Cigars.

Figure 3.1: Menu of the Century Club dinner to Mr Wilkie Collins, 1 October 1873; front (The Pierpont Morgan Library, New York, with permission).

The *World* continued, 'The festive good cheer and lively talk continued so long that the dinner seemed likely to end without the usual accompaniment of speechmaking'.[35] A sense of the merriment was revealed on a menu that had been circulated for the purpose of collecting the 'autographs of the company'.[36] It appeared that Collins started the menu circulating by signing his name, followed by the other guests. Eventually the menu came back to him and he signed it again, followed by several others who did the same. Eight names were repeated until, sometime during the festivities, the mistake was noticed (Figure 3.2).

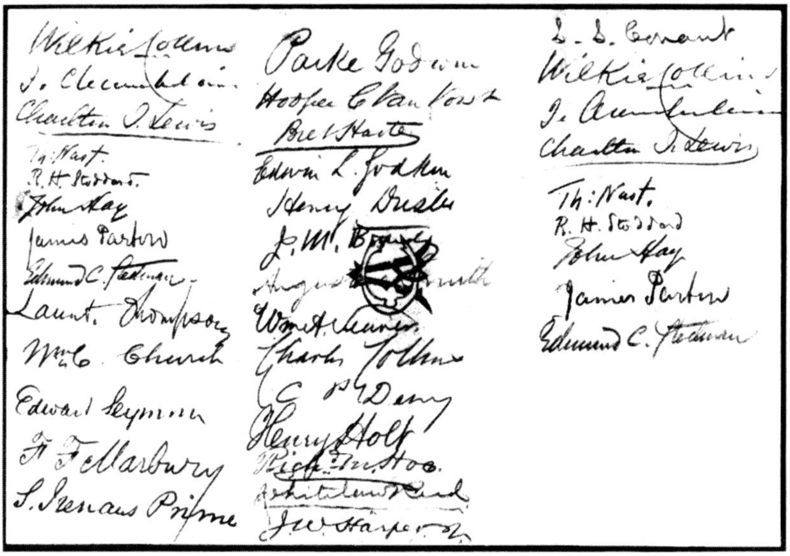

Figure 3.2: Menu of the Century Club dinner to Mr. Wilkie Collins, 1 October 1873; rear (The Pierpont Morgan Library, New York, with permission). The guests in attendance at the Century Club dinner signed the back of the menu. Note that Collins's signature is the first to repeat as the menu starts to circulate for a second time.

At length, 'at a very late hour', the prominent political cartoonist, Thomas Nast, proposed a toast to the guest of honour that was acknowledged by Collins with a few words. Parke Godwin then gave a humorous speech that elicited 'hilarious applause'[37] and others followed. It was observed by the reporter that Collins himself inspired hearty good cheer in those in his presence.

The following day, Collins fled to Fechter's farm. The *New York Daily Graphic* was sympathetic in its announcement:

> Wilkie Collins has had more invitations to read than there are nights to read in and the only way he could escape from the manifold temptations of New York hospitality was to run away with Fechter, to his farm down in Pennsylvania.[38]

Charles Fechter had recently purchased his farm of fifty acres, located half a mile from the village of Richlandtown in Bucks County, about fifty miles from Philadelphia.[39] The retreat that he offered Collins was a small, unassuming stuccoed house on the side of the road, but it was a place where Collins could unwind with his old friend, without intrusion from admirers or the press. He stayed with him for several days, relaxing and preparing for the first of his readings in Albany, New York.[40] He later wrote in a tribute to Fechter that he regretted 'that public engagements limited me to a sojourn of a few days only'.[41]

4 THE TOUR BEGINS: UPSTATE NEW YORK

Rather than travelling directly to Albany from New York City, Collins made arrangements to go by train to Highland Falls, a town on the Hudson River about fifty miles away. He wanted to pay a visit to his old friends Jane and John Bigelow at their country estate, The Squirrels. He had met the couple in London at a dinner party given by Dickens's biographer John Forster in 1867 and had continued a friendly correspondence with them, particularly Jane, over the years.[1] The Bigelow's home in Highland Falls was later described in the local paper:

> 'The Squirrels' looks out over the Hudson River, a quiet, charming old house, with lawns that sweep to the steep cliff's edge. Far below and at one's very feet, West Shore trains dash, slowing up for their stop at Cranston's on the riverbank under this same hill.[2]

In a letter dated 30 September 1873, John Bigelow wrote to Henry Huntington,[3]

> Wilkie Collins has come to give his American cousins reading lessons this winter and from a note rec. since this letter was commenced, I learn that he expects to spend the night of the 6th with us on his way to Albany where he is 'to open' on the 7th.[4]

Bigelow gave a colourful description of Collins's visit to The Squirrels in his diary. In his entry for Tuesday, 8 October[5] he wrote,

> Went up to meet Collins by the 5.40 pm train. It rained and blew as if it never expected another chance. To my surprise he came, but did not bring his baggage so I had to send Odell up after them.

After a description of fellow dinner guests, Bigelow continued,

> Collins enjoyed his dinner but his brandy after it, yet more. He says Benzon is dead. Forster he thinks more hipped [*i.e.* depressed] than sick. His Life of Dickens worries him because of the [*illegible*] it has provoked. It presents the selfishly appearing side of Dickens's character because it seems to be Forster's plan to give only his letters. C. [Collins] has got many which Forster proposed to use if he could use them in the

same way but that did not suit Wilkie and he retains them. C. [Collins] says he has a letter from D. [Dickens] explaining his reasons for separating from his wife. He thinks Forster very injudicious in publishing what D. [Dickens] says about his mother who after all behaved quite sensibly in insisting that her boy should contribute towards the family support by sticking labels on blacking bottles so long as that was the best remunerated work he could do. Collins said he would not have published these letters. Flora [Bigelow's daughter] took a great fancy to Collins and he to her. I took him to the wharf at 12 am today & sent him on to Albany where he reads tonight. Should the weather not improve his reception in Albany will not be very encouraging.[6]

Albany and Troy, New York

Collins departed by steamboat from Cozzen's Wharf, directly below The Squirrels, completing the 100-mile trip to Albany by afternoon. He checked into the Delavan House Hotel where he rested and prepared for that evening's performance.

In spite of the unpromising weather that Bigelow had foreseen, 'every desirable seat at Martin Hall was taken'.[7] At 8.00, Collins 'tripped across the stage' to 'hearty applause'.[8] President Littlefield, of the Young Men's Association of Albany, introduced the speaker 'with a few well-chosen words', after which Collins 'made a beaming bow'. Before he began his reading, Collins remarked that the story, 'The Dream Woman', had been revised and amplified for the purpose of his readings. He added,

> In the hour and a half in which I shall have the honor of appearing before you this evening, you can judge for yourselves whether or no I have succeeded in making it entertaining.[9]

He then opened his manuscript and began to read. A reviewer enthusiastically described the effect that the reading had on the audience, in spite of a 'threatening fire' that broke out nearby at Anthony & McLaren's Machine Shop at 10.05 p.m.[10]

> It would be impossible to bring together a better representation of the lovers of fine literature and more cultivated minds than greeted Mr. Collins. The mental quality of the audience and the power of the reader in holding the attention of his listeners was well shown by the perfect composure with which an alarm by the fire bells was taken – it seemed really to be considered only a little impertinence and was not heeded.[11]

Collins himself was very pleased. In a letter to dramatist Dion Boucicault[12] he exclaimed, 'The story so rivetted [*sic*] the audience that not a soul stirred – and even when there was an alarm of the fire in the neighborhood, and the alarm-bell ringing outside!'[13] Perhaps the rapt attention that Collins was able to capture from his audience came from the fact that 'there was no flourish, no bluster, and the audience forgot the reader in his subject'.[14]

The following day, Collins 'received various courteous attentions'. Mr Littlefield took him on a drive and showed him the sights of Albany. He met with the Governor of New York, John Dix. Later, he was entertained at a reception at the home of Col. Frederick T. Martin, former president of the Young Men's Association, where many 'distinguished citizens' were given the opportunity to meet the great novelist.[15] As the *Albany Argus* concluded,

> If Mr. Collins meets with such appreciative listeners throughout the country, as he has found in Albany, it will be no less than a gratification to him than to us that he has come to America.[16]

In his letter to Boucicault, Collins wrote that, after Albany, he was scheduled to 'go on reading in this State, and perhaps at Philadelphia', returning to New York City on 21 October. He wrote another letter from Albany, to the New York banking house of Duncan Sherman, in which he enclosed two cheques to be paid to his credit: one for $525 on the Bank of North America and one for $270.66 on Albany County Bank. The cheques may have been an advance from the American Literary Bureau and a portion of the admission proceeds from the previous night.

The same afternoon he departed for Troy, New York, ten miles by train from Albany. Following the same pattern as in Albany, he checked into the Troy House and prepared himself for his evening performance at Rand's Hall.

At 8.00 he walked on stage before a 'cultured, if not overflowing audience'. Although The *Troy Daily Press* described the story as 'remarkable', 'weird and powerful in plot', and 'graphic and beautiful in style', it conceded that, as a reader, Collins was 'no actor, and only the thrilling nature of the story redeemed his reading from dullness', because he was 'far from being an elocutionist'.[17]

A further review appeared the following day, but was no more affirmative. It described 'an utter absence of vivacity' in the reading and included such words as 'tedium', 'monotony' and 'tameness'. The review was hardly kinder in regards to Collins as a writer. Although it referred to him as 'power in the land', it lamented that his plots were 'without much regard to probability' and his characters were 'the like of whom are seldom met with in actual life'. It went on to attack Collins's newest novel, *The New Magdalen* as 'a lamentable failure' and continued to rant,

> but there is something so improbable, so unnatural, and so widely at variance with our ideas and experience of social life, in a reformed London street-walker – certainly a *very* new Magdalen – fascinating a brilliant and eminent clergyman by the common, sympathetic clap-trap narrative of her wrongs and at length winning his heart and

> hand in lawful marriage, and securing the ardent affection of a virtuous lady of rank, that we feel like throwing the book down in disgust.[18]

In spite of the negative review of *The New Magdalen* as a book, the *Troy Daily Press* highly praised the dramatic performance of the same work at the Opera House on the night following his reading. The theatre review referred to 'Wilkie Collins' thrilling story' and extolled the 'sterling artists' Annie Firmin and John Jack, who performed the starring roles.[19]

The reviewer for the *Troy Daily Times* was more positive about 'The Dream Woman', saying the hall should have been filled, for those who did not attend 'missed a most enjoyable entertainment – a good story'. As for Collins himself, the reviewer wrote that Collins 'was very much pleased with the audience', and quoted him as saying, 'the Troy people were appreciative'. No doubt Collins's pleasure was enhanced by his receipt of three-fourths of the evening's gross receipts, which the reviewer considered 'too large a share'.[20]

On 13 December 1873, Collins wrote to J. [F.] Thompson to thank him for having given him in Troy a printed pamphlet recounting the true case of *The Trial of Jesse and Stephen Boorn* (Figure 4.1). Collins acknowledged that his story *John Jago's Ghost, or The Dead Alive*, which commenced publication in the *New York Fireside Companion* on 29 December 1873, 'was based on the main facts of the case'.[21] Following its review of Collins's reading of 'The Dream Woman' on 8 October 1873, the *Troy Daily Press* noted in the 'Personal' section, 'Capt. J. F. Thompson, formerly of the One Hundred and Sixty-ninth Regiment, was in town [the same day]'.[22] It is probable that Captain Thompson gave the pamphlet to Collins following the 8 October reading.

On the morning after his reading, Grant Thompson, Corresponding Secretary of the Young Men's Association, gave Collins a tour of Troy before his departure on the 2.00 train for Utica, New York.[23]

Utica and Syracuse, New York

Collins arrived in Utica, located 100 miles west of Troy, on the afternoon before his reading. That morning the *Utica Morning Herald* ran a long article about Collins containing his biography, a personal sketch and a chronology of his works. The article appears to have been intended to generate interest in that evening's performance and enhance the sale of tickets substantially more expensive than competing Utica entertainments. Tickets to 'The Dream Woman' sold for $0.75 and $1.00 while tickets to other advertised 'Entertainments', such as the 'eminent comedian' J. H. Stoddart or 'Scenery of Ireland' went for $0.35 to $0.75.

Perhaps the tickets were too expensive, as Collins attracted 'a paltry four hundred, at the most generous estimate' to his reading at the Opera House on

THE

TRIAL, CONFESSIONS

AND CONVICTION

OF

JESSE AND STEPHEN BOORN,

FOR THE MURDER OF

RUSSELL COLVIN,

AND

THE RETURN OF THE MAN SUPPOSED TO HAVE BEEN MURDERED.

By Hon. LEONARD SARGEANT.

Ex-Lieut. Governor of Vermont.

MANCHESTER, VT.:
JOURNAL BOOK AND JOB OFFICE.
1873.

Figure 4.1: Collins based *The Dead Alive* on facts of a case recounted in a pamphlet presented to him in Troy (Author's collection).

that evening. The reviewer was at a loss to account for 'such apathy on the part of our amusement seekers and literati'.[24]

According to a review the next day, Collins's voice was low and pleasant, with an unmistakably British accent. The cadence, however, seemed to put stress on unimportant words and give a 'peculiar rising inflection' at the end of sentences. There was little variety to his tone and all of his characters sounded much the same. The reviewer stated that he was 'no elocutionist', but rather it was the narrative, not the delivery, that kept the listener's interest. Fortunately, the review concluded, 'the reader is soon forgotten, and the novelist is all we hear'.[25]

Collins departed Utica on 10 October and continued west across upstate New York to Syracuse, a distance of fifty-five miles. Wybert Reeve, in his 'Recollections of Wilkie Collins', relates 'an amusing circumstance' that once again illustrated the American customs that Collins observed as strange. This incident occurred in 'an up-country town' that might well have been Syracuse. Reeve related that Collins had arrived in the afternoon to give a reading in the evening, and was washing himself after a long railroad journey. He continued,

> when a nigger servant in the hotel opened the door of his bedroom without knocking, and asked:
>
> 'Are you the Britisher as is come down 'ere to do a bit o' reading?'
>
> 'Yes, I suppose I am the man.'
>
> 'Well, 'ere's some o' the big bugs and bosses o' this 'ere town come jist to see you.'
>
> Some of the chief men in the town had come to pay their respects and welcome him.
>
> 'That's awkward,' replied Collins; 'I am just dressing.'
>
> 'I guess they'll wait till you've scrubbed your skin and put on your pants. Jist say when you're ready.'
>
> With that he coolly walked to the window, opened it – it was a very cold day – and leaning out, commenced leisurely spitting into the yard below. He was chewing tobacco.[26]
>
> 'My friend,' said Collins, 'when you have done spitting, would you mind closing that window?'
>
> 'Well, I don't see the harm it's a-doing you.'
>
> 'Perhaps not; but if you will shut it, and tell the gentlemen below I will be with them directly, it will do me more good.'
>
> 'You'd better tell them yourself, I guess. If you objects to my spitting out o' this winder, I objects to yer trying to boss this establishment. So jist you tell 'em yerself;' and putting his hands in his pockets, he leisurely lounged out of the room.[27]

On Saturday, 11 October, Collins gave a reading at the Wieting Opera House, again sponsored by the Young Men's Christian Association, the president of which, a Mr Hanchett, introduced him. It was reported that when Mr Hatchett started to describe him in superlatives, Collins interrupted him and quipped, 'Don't introduce me as the greatest living novelist. I've been introduced so a number of times, and I'd rather be simply Mr. Collins. You know, everybody is the greatest living something.'[28]

The evening was not a success, the *Syracuse Courier* bluntly stating, 'As a reader, Mr. Collins is unquestionably a failure'.[29] The enthusiastic reports of his talents that had preceded his performances in Albany and Troy were being replaced by more accurate assessments. Although his skills as a novelist were never contested, on the stage, he was no Dickens.

Two days before he was scheduled to deliver his Syracuse reading, the local paper carried a quote from the *Albany Express* that described Collins, the reader, as 'easy, graceful and finished, his principal merit being the great intensity with which he impresses the hearer'.[30] Ads touted 'The Dream Woman' as a 'Most Fascinating Novelette'. But the people of Syracuse did not respond and only a small audience turned out. The *Syracuse Daily Standard* attributed the disappointing attendance to the fact that

> 'The Dream Woman' ... lacks that heart interest that reaches out and enlists continuous sympathy and attention. This idea had preceded the great novelist, from criticisms in other places, and accounted in great part for the small audience here.[31]

The review in the *Syracuse Journal* was dismal. After a rather dismissive synopsis of the story, the reviewer added,

> A dreariness and weariness come over the audience and force the wish that the climax, whatever it may be, may soon be reached. The voice of the reader becomes monotonous ... As a reader he suffers by the criticisms fully made during his interval of rest at the conclusion of the second chapter, and when he reappears the applause is less noticeable than when he is introduced.[32]

The price of tickets had also become an issue in Syracuse. The *Syracuse Daily Courier* reported that tickets for reserved seats would be available for as much as a dollar. A disclaimer followed this announcement:

> The Young Men's Christian Association is not responsible for this, as it is expressly stipulated in Mr. Collins' contract that this should be the price.[33]

The *Syracuse Journal* placed the blame squarely on Collins's manager:

> We cannot but think that Mr. Collins is making a mistake by which his reputation will suffer in making a tour of this country as a reader, especially if he continues his engagement with the Lecture Bureau, which by its prices seems to hold him in so much higher estimation than is the case with the public.[34]

Public sensitivity to ticket prices was undoubtedly exacerbated by the panic affecting financial centres in the United States, as banks and trust companies failed.[35] The issue was met head-on in the *Daily Courier*'s review of Collins's performance:

> The natural carefulness of the public in money matters at the present time may have influenced some, but the main cause is directly traceable to the Lecture Bureau under whose auspices Mr. Collins came to this city. The agents of the bureau had been repeatedly warned that no lecturer or reader, however popular, could draw a large audience in this city if the price of tickets was raised. In spite of this warning, they persisted in bringing Mr. Collins here and doubling the price of tickets, instead of engaging him to some lecture committees who are familiar with this locality. The people of this city will not submit to extortion, even to see Mr. Wilkie Collins.[36]

Word of the criticism of the Syracuse reading reached Buffalo, where Collins was scheduled for a later appearance. A paper there described the issue of ticket prices and the disappointing evening, but offered a different explanation:

> It is our private opinion, however, that the people of Syracuse were not able to fully appreciate Mr. Collins without a New York [City] entertainment. If the distinguished novelist has started out boldly in the metropolis and achieved success, the prestige thus gained would have brought him good houses in Syracuse, and possibly elsewhere.[37]

Collins's early concerns about Mr Brelsford and the American Literary Bureau were becoming justified.

A Change of Plans

Collins clearly anticipated reading in Rochester, New York on 13 October. While in Albany, he had written his bank in New York City to forward mail to his Rochester hotel. The local papers ran ads that 'Wilkie Collins will be appearing at Corinthian Hall on Monday evening, October 13'. Tickets were available at Dewey's Bookstore for $1.00 for all seats.[38] However, on the scheduled day of the reading, the Rochester newspapers carried the following succinct announcement:

> The sudden illness of Wilkie Collins at Syracuse on Sunday [October 12] renders the POSTPONEMENT of his recital in Corinthian Hall this evening absolutely necessary. A new date will be announced within a few days. Ticket holders will please be patient until the Agent arrives in the city.
>
> AMERCIAN LITERARY BUREAU[39]

The following evening, reports were more expansive.[40] Charles Brelsford had sent letters to the newspapers, offering an explanation.

> A letter from C. M. Brelsford, President of the American Literary Bureau, under whose auspices the engagement of Wilkie Collins is conducted, states that the cause

> of the novelist's illness is nervous prostration and a severe cold, affecting his voice. Hereafter he will give his entertainments only on alternate days. The management announces its desire to carry forward the engagement of Corinthian Hall to some future date.

The cancellation and the explanation for it gave the reporter the opportunity to express opinions that had been growing more pronounced at each of Collins's venues:

> When Mr. Collins will appear here is, therefore, a matter of uncertainty, and grave doubts are expressed as to whether he will come at all. His lectures in Troy, Utica, Syracuse and elsewhere have not been successful pecuniarily, and some of the journals boldly pronounce him a failure as a reader. One thing is certain – the price of tickets – one dollar – is much too high for such an entertainment, and people will not pay it to hear or see any literary man. Lecture speculators may well understand this first as last. If Mr. Brelsford intends to bring Wilkie Collins to this city and desires a good house he must reduce the admission to fifty cents. At one dollar he would not be likely to sell one hundred and fifty tickets. The public willingly submit to extortionate prices, when the object is to raise a charitable fund, but when a private money-making enterprise makes excessive demands they are not cheerfully acceded to.[41]

It is not known where Collins went from Syracuse. According to one report, Mr. Charles Mumford of the New York Literary Bureau had arranged for him to read at Williamsport, Pennsylvania, 180 miles south of Syracuse, on 15 October.[42] Although there is no report that this appearance actually took place, he could easily have read there and still travelled the additional 180 miles to Philadelphia in time for his reading on 17 October.

It is, however, equally possible that Collins returned to New York to rest and regroup. Word began to circulate throughout the States that the great novelist was suffering. 'Wilkie Collins had been ill', announced the *New York Daily Graphic*.[43] 'Wilkie Collins' health is so poor that he can only appear on alternate evenings', proclaimed the *Daily Constitution* of Middleton, Connecticut.[44] The *Dubuque Herald* at first made light of things, jokingly suggesting,

> The cause of Wilkie Collins's sickness is said to be the statement of one of his American acquaintances, in his presence, that he looked like the picture on the 50-cent scrip.[45]

A week later it proposed,

> Wilkie Collins has abandoned his lecture engagements, because of serious prostration, which means probably that he has failed.[46]

The *Buffalo Express* reported,

> Mr. Collins was to have given one of his readings in Rochester on Monday evening but a telegram was received in that city on Sunday stating that on account of sudden illness he would be unable to fulfill his engagement ... We trust Mr. Collins will not fail to visit Buffalo.[47]

Years later, Collins still recalled the discomforts of American rail travel and its effect on his constitution:

> I remember once, after two days' and a night's traveling, I was so utterly worn out that I asked the landlord of the hotel if he had any very dry champagne. He replied that he had. 'Then' I said, 'send a bottle up to my bedroom'. I drank the whole of it, and informed him that though it was only noon, I was going at once to bed, and that all visitors were to be told that I might possibly not get up for a week. I heard afterwards that after twenty-four hours some callers were allowed to come up and peep in at the door, which I had not locked; but all they saw was 'Mr. Collins still fast asleep'.[48]

5 READINGS AND RESPONSES: PHILADELPHIA, BOSTON AND NEW YORK

Collins had a well-publicized reading scheduled in Philadelphia, Pennsylvania, on 17 October. His was to be the inaugural programme in a series of 'literary and musical entertainments' at Horticultural Hall. The series included such headliners as Harriet Beecher Stowe, the controversial Charles Bradlaugh, Rev. Henry Ward Beecher and Mrs. Scott Siddons, who was to give Shakespearian readings in costume. Tickets for each performance were available at $0.50 for general admission and $0.75–$1.00 for reserved seats, or $5.00 for the whole series of nine. Thus Collins was not only to introduce the series, but tickets could be economically purchased for nine evenings of entertainment, including 'pleasant musical interludes in connection with each'.[1]

The Philadelphia newspapers anticipated the reading, citing the positive report from Albany and adding,

> We await anxiously his arrival in Philadelphia, an event which is now happily close at hand. It would content us only to look at and listen to one who has so often been the companion of a solitary hour, or the delight of a social one, while from the printed page he told some strange story.[2]

Everything appeared favourable for a successful performance. On Friday evening, 17 October, the hall was full to overflowing, with many forced to occupy seats on the stage. The audience consisted of 'persons of note ... in social and literary circles'.[3] As the *Philadelphia Press* put it,

> No better proof could have been given of the popularity of his writings than this unusual gathering of intelligent people. Nor could anything be more hearty than their welcome when he made his appearance. It reminded us of the honors to Dickens.[4]

As advertised, the evening began with musical entertainment. Liszt's 'Wedding March' was followed by a violin and piano duet of 'William Tell'. Finally, 'the curiosity of the vast assemblage was gratified' at 8.00 when Collins appeared on the platform.[5] He made a few introductory remarks:

> Ladies and Gentlemen: I have no pretensions to appear as an actor or elocutionist, but simply to read my story before a large parlor of, I hope I may say, friends, and then leave it to rest on any merits it possesses.[6]

The reading was not a success. The *Philadelphia Press* report was devastating:

> The favor of the audience diminished as the reading progressed. Making every allowance for his disclaimer that he is neither an actor nor an elocutionist, it is clear that Mr. Collins can never gain the sympathy of his hearers ... But the chief defect was the absence of anything like a broad and genial humanity. Dickens provoked alternate tears and laughter ... Edmund Yates was brusque and genial ... and we left them ... feeling that we had enjoyed and learned something. But Mr. Collins disappointed everybody; for everybody liked his written novels, and came prepared to like his spoken ones.

Concerning 'The Dream Woman', the review continued,

> Not to seem hypercritical with one so prominent in literature, it is also true that his story was not a good story in a singular particular. It was not even a fair sensation. The dream was no dream. The situations were unreal. There was no humor, and nothing new. And, more than all, the moral was just as bad as bad could be. It was not pleasant to hear a famous Englishman describing, before several hundred pure girls, how one wretched, fallen woman, after mysteriously killing her man, had captivated two more, and stabbed another to death in a drunken frenzy. Philadelphia is always glad to greet men of letters, come from where they may, and Mr. Collins has been specially honored as a first-class manufacturer of sensations; but he is not a reader, and, even if he were, what he has written for the platform is not fit for intelligent and cultivated people.[7]

Two days later, a letter to the editor further reinforced the *Press*'s review.

> *To the Editor of the Press:*
>
> Sir: In the name of the wives and daughters of Philadelphia, I desire to thank you for your fearless and just criticism of Mr. Wilkie Collins' lecture of Friday evening, which must have been considered by every lady present as an insult. Never having admired the works of this gentleman, I went willingly to hear him, trusting that I should be so agreeably entertained as to be inspired with new interest in his productions; but a few minutes sufficed to convince me that the composition was not only of a low order, but unsuited in every particular to the taste and requirements of a refined and appreciative audience.
>
> The manner of the reader was not calculated to leave a pleasing impression, but it is not my purpose to dwell upon that point, although, as to dullness, I do not remember its equal since G. P. R. James many years ago introduced his solitary horseman to the public from an American platform. There was nothing in it that could refresh the spirit, exalt the thoughts, awaken reflections, or invite research. There was nothing to encourage the young to noble effort, or to rouse the sympathies towards suffering humanity, nor were there deficiencies compensated for by an approach to wit or humor. We would have guarded our children, if possible, against reading such an

immoral book, yet, in the lecture room, the favorite and safe resort of many families, they were compelled to listen to that which was low in its tendency, and utterly without moral.

If visitors from other lands wish to be kindly remembered after leaving our shores, they must provide a different sort of aliment for our intellectual entertainment from that which Mr. Collins has brought, for they will assuredly find that we are capable of enjoying nothing but the highest and best and will not rest satisfied with what they may choose to bestow, however unworthy.

Again thanking you for the candid remarks in today's issue, I must express the hope that you will carefully watch over the interests of the lecture platform, and guard us from similar impositions.

Respectfully, Caroline
Philadelphia, October 18, 1873.

In the end, however, it seemed that Collins's acceptance that night depended upon the ear – and the taste – of the listener. For while the *Press* insisted that Collins's 'voice is unfortunately too low for our great halls, and too monotonous to stir and hold public attention',[8] the *Philadelphia Inquirer* claimed that 'Mr. Collins read in a very clear and distinct voice being heard in every portion of the large hall. He possesses the desirable faculty of keeping his audience fascinated and interested'.[9] One can only hope that Collins was presented with solely the review of the *Inquirer* with his coffee the next morning.

The following Sunday, Collins was entertained by George Childs,[10] publisher of the *Philadelphia Public Ledger*. Childs and Collins first became acquainted through their mutual association with Dickens years earlier. In his *Recollections,* Childs described Collins as 'one of the most agreeable men I ever met'.[11]

Back to New York

From his rooms at the Westminster Hotel in New York City, Collins wrote a letter to Childs dated 21 October. He thanked his host for 'the delightful evening',[12] as a guest of Childs and his wife at their Philadelphia home. Sometime later, he reminisced in another letter about dining with the Childs 'in that beautiful room, at that well-spread table'.[13]

Collins regretted that he would not be able to accompany the Childs on a 'mountain trip' (possibly to the Pocono Mountains area west of New York City) because of reading dates that necessitated his being in Boston by Tuesday, 28 October. He also referred to a consultation after his return to New York, commenting to Childs that he had been 'medically advised to limit my railway traveling as much as possible' in conjunction with 'the strain of these public readings'.[14]

The *New York Tribune* reported that 'Wilkie Collins has returned from the provinces to be exposed once more to the exacting hospitality of New York',[15] and indeed, he was. Wednesday morning, 22 October, Collins was honoured at an elegant, but spirited, breakfast banquet at the Union Club on Fifth Avenue. The affair was hosted by Col. William Seaver of *Harper's Magazine*,[16] whom he had met by a letter of introduction from Edmund Yates.[17] An indication of the mood of the gathering is garnered from an exchange between Seaver and John Hay:[18]

October 18, 1873

My dear Hay,

Come to me on the 22nd at Union Club, at 12 n. and help thrust a swell breakfast down the throat of Wilkie Collins, That's a good child.

Affectionately,

Wm A. Seaver[19]

October 20, 1873

My dear Seaver,

I have just received your letter and will help you in your enterprise of the 22nd. The G.L.N. must eat that breakfast, or 40 millions of free men shall know the reason why. Shall I bring a sausage stuffer or will you provide them?

Yours,

John Hay[20]

According to one report, 'some dozens of the best known people in the city were present' including William Cullen Bryant, Oliver Wendell Holmes[21] and Connecticut Governor Charles Ingersoll.[22] It was a merry affair, and 'neat and witty speeches were made by many of the participants'.[23]

Collins remained in New York for the next five days, writing letters, meeting with friends, tolerating admirers and trying to rest when he could.

First Boston Reading

On Tuesday, 28 October, Collins arrived in Boston[24] 'in good health'[25] although in bad weather. Most of October had been unseasonably stormy and even when it was clear, it was cold.[26] However, he responded favourably to the American climate, commenting later, 'America suits me much better as a climate to live in than England'.[27] He settled into his rooms at the Tremont House on the corner of bustling Tremont and Beacon Streets, where Dickens had stayed on his first tour in 1842.[28]

A flurry of pleasant social activity began as soon as he arrived. His first night in Boston, he dined at the home of James T. Fields, publisher and past editor of *Atlantic Monthly*, and his wife Annie, whom he met previously through Dickens. After dinner, they took him to the opera.[29] Collins considered the Fields to be good friends, but he might have felt differently had he known what Annie later wrote in her diary:

> Saturday, Nov. 1 – Last Tuesday, I have omitted to set down our first visit from Mr. Wilkie Collins – a small man with an odd figure and forehead and shoulders much too coarse for the rest of him – His talk was rapid and pleasant but not at all inspiring – He appears to be quick at adapting plays for the stage; a kind of superior Bouricault. A man who has been much feted and fatted in London society who has overeaten and overdrunk and has been ill, is gouty and in short is no very wonderful specimen of a human being.[30]

Perhaps Annie's opinion of Collins had been unfairly influenced by a mean-spirited letter she had received from Dickens's sister-in-law, Georgina Hogarth:

> Wilkie Collins is going to America in September – you shall see him no doubt – I have but the slightest idea whether he is likely to be successful or not – I have heard he is to read but I cannot imagine his reading well. He seems to me to have no physical qualification for it – I forget whether you know him? He is agreeable and easy to get on with – and he has many fine qualities but he has an unusual amount of conceit and self-satisfaction – and I do not think any one can think Wilkie Collins a greater man than Wilkie Collins thinks himself ...[31]

Collins gave his first Boston reading on the evening of 30 October at the Music Hall, a huge venue with a seating capacity of 2,585 and ranking as 'among the finest and largest public halls in the world'. The interior was grand and imposing and the acoustic properties were said to be remarkable.[32] His reading was arranged as part of the Old Bay State Lecture series, of which Charles Bradlaugh was also a part. Tickets for the single event were $1.00[33] but had been selling well.

By 7.30, the house was filled with 'many of our most distinguished citizens'[34] gathered to hear the great novelist. Richard Proctor, the eminent astronomer who himself was lecturing in the principal cities of the United States, was seated on the crowded platform.[35] Mr Roberts, representing Old Bay State, gave the introduction. Collins spoke for more than two hours, with a short intermission 'for the repose of the audience and the reader'.[36]

Although the *Boston Globe* reported, 'the critical and refined audience ... watched every motion [and] weighed every word', it noted that a 'considerable' number of people left before the end. This, however, was attributed to the fact that as residents of the suburbs, they 'were obliged to hasten, or miss their homeward trains'.[37] Those who stayed 'an hour beyond the usual time of a popular lecture' were, according to the *Boston Evening Transcript*, all 'so wide awake that there was not one "Dream Woman" in the hall'.[38]

The *Boston Commonwealth* warmly noted that Collins 'evidently feels heart in his work, and his sincere earnestness, although unobtrusive, was deeply impressive'[39] and the *Boston Evening Traveller* expressed an opinion frequently shared in other reviews:

> No man is more deserving of enthusiastic reception here than the author of 'The Moonstone' and of 'Armadale,' who has contributed so largely to the sum of human enjoyment.[40]

Later, the review in the *Commonwealth* was cause for a good laugh for Collins and his friend Wybert Reeve. Referring to Collins's voice, the reporter made the comment, 'the London intonation is noticeable occasionally in a flattening of the vowels'. According to Reeve, the review was then copied into a Western paper, which said, 'Our contemporary in Boston says Mr Collins is decidedly a Londoner, which is apparent in the flattening of his *bowels*'.[41]

On Friday, Collins made an excursion to nearby Cambridge, possibly to sit for a photographic portrait by the well-known Boston photographer, George Kendall Warren. He returned to Boston for a dinner engagement, probably at the home of Sebastian Schlesinger,[42] a relative of Fred Lehmann who had introduced the two by letter. Described by Collins as a 'bright little fellow', Schlesinger was a man of many talents. Besides serving as German Consul in Boston, he was an accomplished music composer, and was employed as an insurance officer at Naylor & Co. where Collins's godson Frank Ward[43] worked for him.[44] The two men immediately took to each other. At first, their relationship was professional, Collins insuring himself through the firm. As their friendship grew, Schlesinger and his wife entertained him often, Collins commenting in a letter to Lehmann that Schlesinger 'wouldn't hear' of his dining at the hotel and that he made 'the best cocktail in America'.[45] Their friendship continued long after Collins returned home, and in 1878 he dedicated *The Haunted Hotel* to 'Mr and Mrs Sebastian Schlesinger, in Remembrance of Much Kindness and of Many Happy Days'.[46]

Busy Days in New York

On Saturday, 1 November, Collins returned to New York,[47] where not only would he be preparing for his first reading in the City, but he would also oversee the authorized American production of his play *The New Magdalen*. Before he left Boston, Collins wrote to Schlesinger:

> I am going to ask you to kindly allow my Godson to pay me a little visit at New York – if you can spare him from the office on Monday and Tuesday, November 10th and 11th? On the first of these dates the dramatic 'New Magdalen' is produced in New York, and on the second, I make my first appearance there as a reader. These are interesting occasions to Frank, and –subject to your approval – I have asked him to stay with me at my hotel.[48]

Ward quickly became invaluable to Collins as a secretary and general assistant, staying on until 16 November. On that day, Collins wrote Schlesinger that Ward would be returning in the evening and requesting that he be allowed to come back to accompany him on his next tour 'to Baltimore and one or two southern towns', adding, 'It will really be doing me a great favor if you will let him come back to me'.[49]

Around this time Collins arranged to sit for a series of photographs by renowned photographer Napoleon Sarony at his Broadway studio. A small man, Sarony was flamboyant and charming, and Collins immediately felt comfortable with him. Sarony assessed Collins's personality and created imaginative poses with special lighting and props, capturing images that were completely natural. The results delighted them both. A reporter for the *Cleveland Plain Dealer* called them 'capital likenesses'.[50] In a later interview, Sarony described his experience of photographing Collins:

> When Wilkie came to me, I discerned a peculiarity of facial expression when he talked about his own books, which was most interesting; so while he kindly answered a question or two for me about his *Woman in White*, I made a quick exposure, feeling that I had taken the great novelist at his best. And so it proved. When he returned to England, he wrote to me: 'You have taken just the sort of photograph I like. Those taken of me over here are perfect libels, but I feel like giving your pictures to all my friends.'[51]

Collins continued to correspond with Sarony long after his departure from America, the photographer occasionally sending samples of his 'art' photographs to an appreciative recipient.[52] In 1883 Collins dedicated *Heart and Science* 'To Sarony (of New York), Artist, Photographer and Good Friend'.[53]

There is some indication at this point that Collins's arrangement with Charles Brelsford and the American Literary Bureau was taking a turn for the worse. In a letter written on 25 October, Collins seemed confused about his schedule:

> So far as I know, at present, I shall read at Providence on November 3rd. But I am also due to read at other places on the 1st and the 5th.[54]

Collins did not speak in Providence on that date, nor is there any indication that he spoke anywhere else around that time. In a letter of 9 November, written from the Westminster Hotel in New York, Collins said that he was 'overwhelmed ... with work and correspondence'. He added, 'My plans are not yet settled for my next trip to Boston – or for my readings to come, in the course of this winter'.[55] That evening, he attended the annual dinner of the Mercantile Library Association, under whose auspices his reading was to be presented. After dinner, he gave a spirited response to a toast to England and America.[56]

During the first week of November, Collins was attending rehearsals for the New York premiere of *The New Magdalen.* On 9 May, four months before Collins's arrival in the United States the play, starring Carlotta Leclercq, had opened at the Globe in Boston, even before its London opening and prior to its publication as a novel. In order to ward off American pirates, Collins had prepared a letter to the actress to be included in the theatre programme:

> If you are threatened with competition on the part of stealers of plays, let the public know that I have reserved scenes and effects for the author's own dramatic version which are not to be found in the novel. I finished the play before I finished the published story. While the prologue and the first act follow that published story closely, the second act (at the end) departs from it altogether, and contains an entirely new situation. The third, and last act, also presents scenes and effects which have been purposely altered and varied in the novel. Thanks to these precautions, the thieves who may plunder me successfully at the beginning of the story will be quite unable to snatch the latter half of it. The one complete dramatic version of the 'New Magdalen' to be seen in America, is the version which I have confided to your care.
>
> WILKIE COLLINS
> London, April 19, 1873[57]

Collins worked with John Augustin Daly,[58] owner of the Broadway Theater, on the New York production, assisting with casting choices and offering suggestions as to staging, acting and other details. The play opened on 10 November, 'with the great attraction of Miss Carlotta Leclercq in the leading role of [reformed prostitute] Mercy Merrick'.[59] The house was packed in spite of the 'unpleasantly cold' evening. Although the audience was so drawn in by the trials of the heroine that at one point, 'there was hardly a dry eye among the ladies ... and many gentlemen were openly weeping', the reviews afterwards were mixed. In particular, H. H. Wood, in the role of Julian Gray, was labelled 'the fly in the ointment',[60] and Miss Leclercq was described as 'too mature and too massive for the part'.[61]

The true star was Collins himself. At the end of the forth act, a chant of 'Collins! Collins!' went up[62] and he was

> summoned by loud applause, stood in a stage box and bowed to the eager multitude. Again summoned, he came upon the stage, leading Miss Leclercq – to whom, with graceful gesture, he referred as the proper recipient of the public homage. Still called, he emerged for the third time, and this time he acknowledged the welcome:
>
> 'Ladies and Gentlemen: I venture respectfully to think that you have heard enough speeches of mine already. [Loud applause.] You have other speeches of mine to hear, in still another act. Permit me, therefore, standing in this place, to make the briefest speech of all – which is, that I respectfully and cordially thank you'.[63]

As 'A Lady Critic' concluded in the *New York Daily Graphic,*

> The sight of him was probably worth as much to the audience as the play, for everyone likes to see the stuff that authors are made of.[64]

Days after the opening performance, varying responses continued to circulate in the newspapers. William Winter, critic for the *New York Tribune,* conceded that the play was 'neatly constructed, and full of telling incidents' but went on to complain that the subject was

> one that ladies and gentlemen cannot discuss, and that seems to us sufficient reason why it should not be obtruded from the stage. The theater is not a dissecting place, nor a place for the examination of social problems.[65]

The *Graphic* determined that in the 'views of political economy which were placed in the mouth of Julian Gray, it is quite evident that ... Mr. Collins is at heart a thorough radical'.[66] An outraged letter from 'Matador' to the *Graphic* protested,

> A play so utterly vicious, so shamefully profligate in its teachings, has never before been produced at a New York theater ... The author of *The New Magdalen* has opened a recruiting office for prostitutes and has made a direct attack upon virtue and honesty. In the whole range of English dramatic literature, there is not a drama so vicious in its teaching, so shameless in its infamous purpose, as *The New Magdalen*. ... A nasty play? If it had been as nasty as the sewers of New York, that would have been a small offense in comparison with the direct and powerful preaching of vice and the sure and steady depreciation of virtue which characterizes *The New Magdalen* throughout. [67]

To which 'A Wife and Mother' wrote a thoughtful rebuttal:

> [The story] tries to point out to us women, wives and mothers the necessity of exercising that charity which is proverbially so universally withheld from an erring or fallen sister.[68]

The play had a three-week run before going on tour to Boston, Brooklyn and other eastern cities.[69] Unauthorized versions, by Walter Binn and others, were also performed throughout the country, some even before the New York premiere. The Fanny B. Price Theatrical Troupe dramatized the story throughout the Midwest,[70] and the Templeton Troupe took its version at least as far west as Reno, Nevada.[71] Despite initial ambivalence, *The New Magdalen* continued to tour for years in the United States, as it did in England.[72]

Pleased by the audience's response to his play, Collins wrote to William Seaver the following morning, 'The public gave us a great reception last night'. Seaver had invited Collins to dinner on opening night, and Collins regretted being otherwise engaged in supporting 'my fair friend The New Magdalen' to the theatre. Apparently Collins was receiving numerous invitations. He mentioned in a letter to Fred Lehman that he had dined with Barthold Schlesinger,[73] and his letter to Seaver mentioned their dinner together on another recent occasion.[74]

On 11 November, after more than six weeks in America, Collins gave his first reading in New York City. In spite of further 'unpromising weather',[75] an audience representing 'the very cream of [New York's] lecture patrons'[76] assembled at

Association Hall. John and Jane Bigelow were there as his guests, as well as 'many lights of the fashionable world' and 'a few prominent members' of the literary field. Mingled among these,

> were large numbers of young ladies, who watched the reader with that steadfast fixity of gaze which only ladies can fasten on a gentleman of literary eminence, whose writings are to them like household words.[77]

Shortly after 8.00, Collins appeared on the platform and was greeted with a 'long and hearty burst of applause'.[78] Reviews afterward, however, were conflicting. While the *New York Times* said of the story,

> It presents briefly nearly all Mr. Collins's strong qualities and peculiarities as a writer of fiction ... his characters are drawn with wonderful distinctness, the language is as incisive and as epigrammatic as in the author's best works,[79]

the *New York Graphic* criticized,

> There is no moral, no object, no purpose served, except the passing away the time in listening to the recital of what is, after all, a feverish and unwholesome story.[80]

The *New York Tribune* described Collins's reading ability in this way:

> He reads very well, with perfect appreciation, with great clearness and distinctness of annunciation, with an adequate degree of dramatic expression ...[81]

However, the *New York Herald* pronounced, 'As a reader Collins is not a success', and further elaborated,

> Some of the audience went to sleep, some arose and left the hall, and expressions of disappointment were numerous. Our opinion is that Mr. Collins has made two mistakes. One consists in reading a piece of trash ... and the other in having assumed that his vast and deserved success as a novelist was sufficient to waft him triumphantly through an enterprise demanding qualities of the very opposite to those he is universally admitted to possess.[82]

It was becoming clear that what filled the halls and precipitated the applause was not the quality of an evening's entertainment, but Wilkie Collins himself: the eminent novelist and the consummate storyteller.

Collins's social engagements continued at a relentless pace in New York, while at the same time he tried to keep to a regular schedule of writing.[83] In a letter to E. P. Hurlbert, whom he had met at Seaver's breakfast, he accepted an invitation to dine at the Manhattan Club on Fifth Avenue on the fifteenth. He added, 'I don't know what leisure time means'.[84]

On 16 November, Collins bid a temporary farewell to Frank Ward, hoping that Schlesinger would allow him to return as soon as possible. He had dinner plans that evening and was in a rush as he signed off a note to Schlesinger, 'Forgive my hurried letter'.[85] In another letter dated 21 November, Collins wrote to George Bentley, forwarding an installment of short stories by Edwin De Leon for possible publication. Again he made reference to his schedule, writing, 'I am only overwhelmed by the kindness of American readers – while I am in New York I have no spare time'.[86] Also on that day, Collins wrote to his London solicitor William Tindell, asking him to look after Martha and their two daughters who, because of landlord problems, were in need of new accommodations. In closing, he added,

> I am thriving in health and in public (as a reader). If my health could stand constant reading I should make a little fortune. But I am obliged to be careful. My reception is wonderful everywhere. I had only five minutes to spare – and they are gone.[87]

In spite of the social commitments of those busy days following the New York reading, Collins was able to finish work on his American story of *The Dead Alive* in time for the Christmas number of the *Fireside Companion*.

6 THE SECOND SWING: BALTIMORE AND WASHINGTON

Collins was delighted when Frank Ward rejoined him for the trip to Baltimore. They took advantage of a new 'Pennsylvania Air Line' rail service between New York and Baltimore/Washington. The scenery along the 200-mile route was said to be among the most beautiful in the country.[1] They checked into the magnificent new Carrollton Hotel on Light Street in Baltimore, built the year before and boasting all the modern conveniences.[2]

The announcement at the centre of the front page of the *Baltimore Gazette* was that Wilkie Collins would be giving his only Baltimore reading on Wednesday, 26 November at the Masonic Temple. The reading was the third entertainment of the Sadler Business College[3] Course and tickets were $1.00.[4] Collins was happily anticipating the evening, writing to John Elderkin,[5] of 'the most encouraging prospects for the reading tonight' as he thanked him for the proofs of *The Dead Alive*.

In 1869, in response to a request from an American correspondent, Wilkie had written a letter including information about his background. In conjunction with his Baltimore appearance, the *Baltimore Sun* published that letter, written to 'a gentleman of Virginia, now of Baltimore':[6]

No. 90, Gloucester Place
Portman Square, W. London
November 18, 1869

Dear Sir,

My life, like the lives of other literary men, is all in my books. I was born in 1824. I was the oldest of the two sons of William Collins, Royal Academician, the celebrated English painter of the coast scenery and cottage life of his native country. I was christened by the name of his dearest friend, the late Sir David Wilkie, another famous painter of the British School. Wilkie was my godfather.

I was educated at a private school of excellent repute, and learned Latin and Greek as well as most of the boys. The only part of my 'education' which has, as I believe, done me any good in later life was given to me by my father, who took me to Italy with him for two years when I was a boy of twelve years of age. Here I learned to observe for myself, and became, as far as a boy could be, associated with all sorts of

> clever people, whom my father's reputation as a painter collected about him. I never went to college, though my father was willing to send me there. The life was not the sort of life for me, after Italy and the artists. I was tried for a few years in a merchant's office, and did my work and hated it. I was taken from commerce and entered as a student at the bar. I am a barrister of Lincoln's Inn, but I never practiced my profession, and never studied it. I was good for nothing, in short, but writing books, and I ended in writing them. How this 'analytical power' which you and other critics find in my novels comes to me I know no more than you do. The only 'rule' I have in writing a work of fiction is at anybody's service. Begin at the beginning, know what the end is before you write a line, and keep the story always going on. With this, and with enormous pains and care, you have the sum total of what I consciously know of my own art as a writer. These few particulars are entirely at your service.
>
> Faithfully yours,
> Wilkie Collins

That night, another large audience assembled at the new Temple Hall on Charles Street. City father John H. B. Latrobe made the introduction.[7] Reviews, however, were restrained: 'The lecturer was listened to with marked attention and interest that frequently expressed itself in applause'[8] and 'It was obvious that the reader created a favorable impression'.[9]

In reviews of his readings, newspapers frequently included a brief re-telling of the story of 'The Dream Woman', but the *Baltimore Sun* put out an extra Bulletin containing the story in fullest detail for those who were not there or wanted a souvenir of their evening with 'the most popular writer in America'.[10]

The following day, Collins explored the city, expressing to a *Sun* reporter

> his surprise at the size of Baltimore, the elegance of some of its homes, the wretchedness of its architecture generally, and the great number of its churches.

He toured Druid Hill Park, probably with John Latrobe, who served as a park commissioner, and was 'delighted with the charming spots which met his eyes at every turn'[11] within its seven hundred acres of natural beauty, through which snaked a series of shaded and diversified walks.[12]

Years after he returned to London, Baltimore continued to have pleasant associations for Collins. Writing to Jane Bigelow on 2 January 1882, he reminisces,

> I too have my agreeable associations with Baltimore. I well remember the lovely women, the pleasant city, the successful public reading of my story, and the hospitable kindness of Mr. Latrobe and the members of his family.[13]

Collins and Ward departed Baltimore with some regret, travelling forty miles to the Nation's Capital on Friday morning, 28 November.[14] His host for the visit was a Mr Philip of the publishing firm of Philip & Solomon, who introduced him to members of the Washington Club at an afternoon gathering prior to his reading at Lincoln Hall that evening. Tickets to the event were again $1.00, compared with $0.50 charged to hear Harriet Beecher Stowe at the same venue.[15]

After his appearance, Mr Philip honoured Collins at a reception at his home. The *Washington Capital* carried a peculiar anecdote pertaining to Collins's presence at the event that was picked up by newspapers all over the country, from New York to Oregon:

> WILKIE COLLINS AND THE INEBRIATED CONGRESSMAN
>
> Poor Philip was taken considerably aback by a new member he invited to his house for an entertainment he gave to Wilkie Collins. The Hon. Lycurgus Leatherlungs, from the Mill Creek Bottoms of Pennsylvania,[16] had been to a dinner party at Welcker's,[17] and was considerably 'sprung' when he reached Mr. Philip's palatial residence. A few glasses of choice old wine there completed his utter ruin. When he was presented to the celebrated English novelist he seized his hand and holding it firmly but affectionately he gazed with intense earnestness into the face of the novelist. At last, finding his words, he said, 'How are you, Milky?' 'I am quite well, sir: how do you do.' 'O, never mind *me*, Milky; I'm all right; member elect from Mill Creek bottoms, and damned glad to see you.' Here Wilkie made an effort to escape, but the M.C. held on. 'I say, old Milky, I know you. I've got all your books and read one every day. I've got "Hard Cash", "The Last of the Barons", the "Lay of the Last Minstrel", and all of 'em.' At this stunning information Wilkie Collins put all his strength into a frantic endeavor to escape. This, however, only resulted in the newly-made member of Congress throwing his arms around the neck of the novelist and kissing him on the end of his intellectual nose. The spectacles disappeared in the struggle, and the entire force of the festive throng was brought to bear to throw poor 'Milky' into the committee of the whole. Next day, on Mr. Philip proposing to escort his distinguished guest to the Capitol, that he might see the Senate and House of Representatives, Wilkie Collins turned pale, and said, with a shudder: 'No, I thank you: rawther not.' And it is an actual fact that this man of genius left Washington without seeing Vinnie Ream's 'Lincoln,'[18]Powell's 'Death of Perry,' or the howling 'Columbus.'[19]

Collins did, at least, see the exterior of the Capitol building, for in the same 1882 letter to Jane Bigelow, he wrote of Washington's unfavourable comparison to Baltimore:

> But comparing the two cities (may I confess it with all humility in a whisper?) I greatly preferred Baltimore. The prodigious streets and 'avenues' at Washington depressed me indescribably – and I never could get over the idea that the enormous cupola of the Capitol was slowly squeezing the weak and attenuated building underneath into the earth from which it had feebly risen.[20]

The following day, he joined actress Maggie Mitchell for a visit to the newly constructed National Theater. Miss Mitchell was to star in the theatre's opening performance on 1 December of *Fanchon, the Cricket* by George Sand. The theatre was state of the art, with electricity used to light the gas throughout the building. The two 'expressed themselves as highly pleased with the appointments of the building', Collins adding that he had seen no theatre more complete in every detail.[21]

7 A CHANGE OF MANAGERS: THE NORTHEAST

At the beginning of December, Collins and Ward returned to their Westminster Hotel rooms in New York City where Ward continued to handle correspondence while Collins involved himself in rehearsals for the upcoming opening of *The Woman in White* at Daly's Broadway Theater. Ward wrote on Collins's behalf to his Canadian publishers, Hunter, Rose, confirming that the first two parts of *The Dead Alive* had been mailed to them from Baltimore, and reminding them that publication must not occur in Canada before the United States number was released, scheduled for 15 December. After publishing in parts, they would be free to issue it in book form.[1] He closed with a reference to Collins's continuing busy schedule.

Problems with the American Literary Bureau persisted. Collins had completed his contracted obligation, having given the readings stipulated under the Bureau's management. During the time of his association with Brelsford, Collins had witnessed numerous examples of the firm's mismanagement: exorbitant ticket prices that affected attendance, booking inconsistencies that caused periods of both impossibly demanding scheduling and long periods of inactivity, delays in the scheduling of readings in New York City that resulted in a lack of credibility as he toured the lesser venues. As Collins wrote to Fred Lehmann,[2] he believed that had been cheated by the American Literary Bureau, although what specifically caused the allegation is not known. He was, therefore, receptive to an offer from James Redpath to take over the arrangement and promotion of his readings. (The American Literary Bureau, however, continued to use his name in their advertisements in various publications for the duration of his stay in the United States.) The contacts and negotiations that preceded the offer are not known, but on 9 December, Collins responded to a letter from Redpath:

> Your letter received. I willingly adopt your suggestion for a percentage. Particulars when we meet. I leave for Boston tomorrow.[3]

James Redpath, a Scottish-born journalist, founded the Boston Lyceum Bureau in 1868.[4] In only a few years, he had built a bureau respected not only by performers and local lyceum committees, but by the other bureaus as well. The *Boston Globe* captured the essence of Redpath's charisma in the following tribute:

> There always lingered about the Redpath Bureau a charm which none of the others possessed ... It had a distinctive character of its own, which was due to the personality of the originator ... No other bureau has brought together in one group so many distinguished persons of various professions, and no one man has ever held the friendship of so many people who radically differed from each other as James Redpath.[5]

Redpath's sense of honour and impeccable character were to be invaluable in maintaining Collins's reputation.

On Wednesday, 10 December, Collins was back in Boston just long enough to check into the St James Hotel on Franklin Square and to meet with Redpath. The following morning he and Ward were on their way to Providence, Rhode Island, a distance of fifty miles.

The early November Providence reading that Collins mentioned in an earlier letter had not materialized, nor was there a reference to a reading on those dates in the Providence newspapers. The *Providence Daily Journal* carried a large advertisement for an evening with Wilkie Collins at the Music Hall on 11 December, the fifth entertainment of the Franklin Lyceum's course. Tickets were $0.75 for reserved seats and $0.50 general admission.

Collins's performance followed an introductory organ concert. He read to an appreciative audience, which, according to the *Journal*, found it 'pleasant ... to hear him read one of his own works, which though short was interesting'.[6] The paper added, 'His style of reading was easy and natural'.

That opinion, however, was not undisputed. Attending that evening was a small group from the local (Quaker) Friends School of Providence. One of the students, a young man by the name of Chalkey Collins, wrote to his brother a few days later,

> Some of the teachers and the seniors went down to hear Wilkie Collins lecture. He read one of his novels entitled the 'Ostler's Dream,' [*i.e.*, 'The Dream Woman'] which I suppose was very interesting to some but I did not think much of it: he read so low that I could not understand some of it. I don't think he did much honor to the name of Collins in the way of reading. One of the teachers, Mattie Reed, who did not go, let me take her ticket for the evening, which saved me fifty cents.[7]

Nonetheless, Collins was delighted with the pecuniary success of his reading. In a letter to his old friend Frederick Lehmann, he later boasted, 'Providence (the city, not the Deity) paid me 400 dollars in spite of the panic!'[8]

Two days later, Collins was back in Boston. His thank you letter to Capt. Thompson for giving him the Boorn Trial story was sent from the St. James on 13 December. There was, therefore, no reasonable way that he could have travelled more than 450 miles to Lockport, New York, a town thirty miles north of Buffalo, for the reading announced in a Buffalo newspaper:

> Wilkie Collins reads in Lockport on the 12th of December.[9]

This was one more indication that scheduling problems were multiplying from his association with Brelsford. These problems were not going unnoticed. The *Boston Commonwealth* lamented:

> As for Wilkie Collins ... why is he not reading, as we were told he would? We seem to be deserted by our readers from abroad; quite abandoned ... Mr. Collins has read, once, twice, three times, and ceased.[10]

This overstatement might have resulted because Collins had been originally scheduled by the American Literary Bureau to read on numerous dates that did not materialize. In addition to his failed appearances in Providence 'and other places' in early November,[11] the following notice appeared in the *Worcester Spy* on 14 November:

> Anglo American Lecture Course
> Owing to the sudden illness of
> Wilkie Collins
> his reading is postponed[12]

A similar announcement was placed in the New Bedford, Massachusetts paper on the 27 November:

> Wilkie Collins Not Coming – A letter from the agent of Mr. Wilkie Collins informs the Lyceum committee that owing to failing health Mr. Collins is obliged to cancel all engagements. The committee regret this exceedingly as they had been repeatedly assured he would not fail them. No pains will be spared to make up for the disappointment of the public who have so generously patronized the Lyceum.[13]

Although Collins had made several appearances in New York, as well as Baltimore, Washington, Providence and Boston, he was unaware that an unauthorized parallel booking schedule by the American Literary Bureau was leaving scores of disappointed – and disgruntled – fans.

Had he realized the extent of the trouble caused by Brelsford and B. W. Williams, the Boston representative of the American Literary Bureau, perhaps he would have retained James Redpath earlier. But with this new start, there was still time to properly arrange readings 'through the Provinces and the Western States'.[14] Redpath wasted no time taking matters in hand. The *Burlington Free Press* reported on 17 December:

> James Redpath of Boston, editor, author and radical, was at Van Ness House last evening, en route to Montreal, where he goes to make arrangements for the readings of Wilkie Collins before the Dominion public.[15]

A reporter for the *Hartford Daily Courant* summed up the current situation:

> The lecture season is practically ended with us. It has been fairly successful and remunerative to the bureaus; but it has not been a great success to the stars that have come here from abroad. Wilkie Collins is, I believe, among the disappointed ones. Mr. Redpath attributes this to the fact that he put his business matters into the hands of the wrong bureau. Mr. Redpath himself has arranged a tour for the novelist now, with the idea that better luck may come of it.[16]

The Woman in White

While his reading itinerary was in the capable hands of the Redpath Bureau, Collins returned to New York. His social activities resumed and he was reported to have attended the opera with notorious wheeler-dealer Jay Gould, whose speculation in the gold market had led to the 'Black Friday' financial panic of 1869.[17]

On 15 December, Collins was present for the opening of the stage production of *The Woman in White.* Although Wybert Reeve had played Hartright for most of its nineteen-week London run, he took over the role of Fosco near its end. He gained additional experience with the role by touring in England as Fosco,[18] and crossed the Atlantic to open the play at Daly's Broadway Theater. In addition to performing, Reeve had re-written and altered part of the drama, with Collins's permission. In the actor's opinion, these changes 'appeared to greatly increase its effect on the public and its strength as a drama'.[19] The play, however, was not particularly successful, and in spite of reduced ticket prices, ran for only two weeks.[20] Perhaps the problem was that the authorized production had to compete with a number of inferior plagiarized productions that had preceded it, or perhaps it was due to the fact that it was, as the *Graphic* described,

> Produced in an extemporary and irregular manner ... [and suffered from a lack of] thorough discipline and coordination of details to the leading object of the play.[21]

On Wednesday, 17 December, Collins was back in Boston for the night, having accepted a dinner invitation at the home of Jere Abbott on Chestnut Street.[22] The following day, he made a quick trip to New Bedford, where he gave a reading that evening to 'one of the largest Lyceum audiences of the season'.[23] Evidently his audience had forgiven him for the cancellation of his November appearance.

The stage properties for Collins's New Bedford reading were described by the reviewer in painstaking detail:

> [Collins stood behind] ... a low, narrow table six feet long, with a light green velvet cover, on which was a small desk a foot and a half high covered with a lusterless

> maroon stuff. Near each end of the table was a high standing gas burner, with an opaque shade.

The reviewer attempted to add a detailed retelling of the story but was unable to relate the ending because he could not hear it. He described Collins's low voice as

> lost in the hubbub caused by the ill-mannered crowd which always rushes out a little before the close of an entertainment.

Defensively, he concluded, 'Some were disappointed in not finding Mr Collins a first-class reader, but they had no call to be'.[24]

While visiting New Bedford, Collins was the guest of William Bradford, an American painter, photographer and explorer who was known primarily for his paintings of ships and seascapes. In spite of those who escaped early from his reading, he expressed himself 'delighted with his audience and the numerous attentions paid him'. He returned to Boston on Friday morning to prepare for his trip north to Canada.[25]

8 THE 'DOUBLE DIFFICULTY': MONTREAL, TORONTO AND BUFFALO

On Saturday, 20 December, Collins and Ward arrived in Montreal for a reading the following Monday evening.[1] Collins wrote to his friend Schlesinger with his impressions of the city, citing the 'slippery walking in the streets' and the 'horrid stenches' at their hotel,[2] the St. Lawrence.[3]

But Collins's real problems in Montreal were not physical. He wrote to Joseph Harper of his 'coup d'état' in changing managers, calling it 'a double difficulty'.[4] Indeed it was. In Montreal, the American Literary Bureau's unauthorized use of Collins's name and Brelsford's presumption in making arrangements without his knowledge or authority were revealed in a series of unpleasant public exchanges, with Redpath taking the hit.

The incident began with advertisements in the Montreal *Gazette* for two events:

For One Night Only!
The Famous English Novelist
MR. WILKIE COLLINS
Will read in
QUEEN'S HALL
Monday Evening, Dec. 22[5]

And

University Literary Society
The Eighth Public Meeting of
this Society will be held, in the
Association Hall, Corner of Craig and Radegonde Streets
on the Evening of Wednesday [*sic*]
the 22nd instant.[6]

On 20 December, a letter was submitted to the *Montreal Herald* from members of the University Society, accusing James Redpath of breach of contract in disregarding his alleged promise to adhere to former arrangements for a reading, and instead scheduling Collins's appearance on the same night as the Society debate.

THE UNIVERSITY SOCIETY AND MR. WILKIE COLLINS / *To the Editor of the Montreal Herald*: Sir – Hearing that Mr. Redpath, of the Boston Lyceum, now in town as Mr. Wilkie Collins' agent, attempts to justify his course by saying that no arrangement for Mr. Wilkie Collins' services were made with him, the undersigned members of the Committee of the University Literary Society beg to state that Mr. Redpath had an interview with the Committee about ten days ago, when the arrangements with several lecturers under Mr. Redpath's charge were discussed, and upon his statement that he would in a few days have the management of Mr. Wilkie Collins' programs, it was distinctly promised by him that when his arrangements would be completed with Mr. Wilkie Collins, the former arrangements for a lecture before the Society *would be adhered to by him.* The Committee therefore consider Mr. Redpath's course, in introducing Mr. Wilkie Collins' lecture on Monday for his, Mr. Redpath's private benefit, to be *a great breach of contract.* The Society's public debate takes place as announced before the intrusion of Mr. Wilkie Collins' reading, on Monday night.

J. J. Maclaren, President, R. C. Fisher, Vice-President, G. J. Jenkins, Treasurer, W. S. Walker, Secretary, C. P. Davidson, M. Lonergan, S. C. Stevenson[7]

Two days later, the *Gazette* printed an outraged letter from a citizen of Montreal supporting the Society, its work, and Canada in general:

TO THE EDITOR OF THE GAZETTE. Sir – I am given to understand that Mr. Redpath, the Lyceum Broker of Boston, has made overtures to the University Literary Society since arrival in Montreal, and since he has announced Wilkie Collins as under his management, why could not Mr. Redpath have made these same terms known to the Society previous to his leaving Boston, and also previous to his announcement of Mr. Collins in the public prints as under his Bureau? Why did not Mr. Redpath call upon the Secretary or some members of the Society and inform them that he had Mr. Collins under his control and was ready to made engagements, which he had promised to do, when he (Mr. R) was in Montreal a few days ago managing Mr. Gough, as I am informed? The University Society has done its work, and that well, and the citizens have an interest in its success and will not stand by and see it snubbed and snuffed out in this manner by any foreign Lecture Bureau. The public have no desire to see their money leaving their city and being carried away by persons who have no interest or stake in Canada, either from New York or Boston, and the sooner that these foreign gentlemen are given to understand that, the better it will be for their own interest. This style of procedure will have undoubtedly a tendency to bring public lecturers into disrepute and disgrace, for it seems to me that money-making should not be the object for which they are given.

Yours, &c., A CITIZEN[8]

In response to the attacks on the character and reputation of both his client and himself, Redpath submitted a lengthy letter of explanation to both newspapers. He began with a paragraph of 'personal statements' by way of introduction, explained the options that he had offered the members of the University Society, and asked the public to judge him on his own merits:

> MR. COLLINS IN MONTREAL / CARD FROM MR REDPATH / SIR – Amateurs always magnify the importance of their position, and no class more than amateur managers. I am too old a manager not to know that the public care nothing about quarrels behind the scenes; that they are interested only in the artist or author for whom the agent acts – modestly and unobtrusively if he understands his business; otherwise, if he has yet to learn it. I have not sought public notice here. I prefer to be known through results only, as in the success which attended Mr. Gough's appearance.
>
> But I trust, not to the courtesy due to a stranger only, but to the love of fair play which characterizes alike the native and colonial Briton, when I ask you to permit me to say and show that the charges of 'gross breach of contract' preferred against me, from the platform on Friday and in the journals of Saturday, respecting the appearance here of Mr. Collins, by Officers of the University Literary Society, are as ungenerous as they are unsupported by facts.
>
> I am tolerably well known in the United States as the manager of the Boston Lyceum Bureau – an agency for lecturers, readers, and musicians, and during five years past, I have made several thousands of contracts with lecture committees in the Republic and the Dominion. No one yet has accused me of breach of contract. Never has a lecturer failed to appear when I agreed that he should appear, unless detained by accident or sickness, or unless the contract was cancelled by mutual consent. Twice only have lecturers refused to do their part of the contract – and in both cases, I notified the committee in advance so that other arrangements were made, and instantly and publicly refused to act as the agent of these gentlemen any longer. I do not travel with lecturers except in rare instances, and then outside of the lyceums, under a special contract.
>
> Pardon these personal statements as they are necessary for a proper understanding of the case.
>
> During my last visit to Montreal, I did NOT (unconditionally) promise, as every member of the committee knows, to place Mr. Collins with the Society. Yet this was the unqualified statement of the President in introducing Mr. Jenkins. On the contrary I distinctly stated that I was not Mr. Collins' agent, had never met nor spoken with him, knew nothing of his views or plans, and therefore could make no agreement for him. I did promise that if Mr. Collins placed himself in my hands as other lecturers do – to be engaged to committees only – they would have the preference in this city, and be enabled to carry out the unauthorized agreement that had been made with them; although made by men who are personally unfriendly to me.
>
> Now, Mr. Collins did not make any contract with me until Monday last [15th], and my agreement with him was that I should personally manage his business – that is, that I should not make engagements for him with committees but travel independently. He told me that he had no engagement whatever, excepting at Toronto; that the American Literary Bureau had acted in violation of their agreement and made an unwarranted use of his name in presuming to make engagements for him anywhere, without his knowledge or consent – especially, (as I find was the case here in Montreal) months beyond the time that his contract with him extended.

With Mr. Collins I made a special contract for the whole country, and by it my conditional agreement with the committee here was necessarily annulled, as that promise was based on the supposition of a *general* contract.

To make a long route for the season, it was necessary that Mr. Collins should begin in Montreal. In fulfillment of my contract, I came here and engaged the hall, and made arrangements for a reading. But when I found that there was ill feeling engendered, I made every proposal toward cooperation with the University Literary Society that was possible without breaking up the campaign that had been planned for Mr. Collins.

1. *I offered to withdraw altogether and let them have Mr. Collins on the same terms that they had made with the American Literary Bureau,* provided they took him on Monday as announced. I offered to remain here and help them, as well as to look after Mr. Collins' interest. A majority objected to this on account of the financial risks.

II. I offered to take all the risk myself, and, in order that their prestige with the public might be saved, and they they might keep good faith with the purchasers of their season tickets, I offered, not at Mr. Collins' expense but my own, to admit them *free*, not announce myself as manager, and advertise the readings as under their auspices.

Before the Committee met I had offered one of the officers to pay the expense of postponing the debate; to keep my own name out of the advertisements and announce the Reading as under the auspices of the Society. That officer himself, with my authority, went to the morning newspapers and changed the advertisement so as to enable the Society to adopt this proposal.

Concessions could go no further unless I should have consented to be bullied – and, a Borderer of Scotch and English ancestry by birth and an American by love, I never allow any one to bully me, because I don't even know how to submit to it.

The ultimatum of these young men was that I should not bring Mr. Collins here at all just now; that I should myself pay all the expenses I had incurred; and that I should introduce him here after my return from the West – under their patronage.

The reason, and the only reason, given for refusing to accept Monday night, under my offer to assume all risks, was that it would interfere with a debate in which certain members of the Society are to appear. I may add that when I engaged the Hall I knew nothing whatever of this debate.

One officer says that I injured Mr. Jenkins' lecture by bringing Mr. Collins after him. The same gentleman and others told me, *before* there was the least thought of bringing Mr. Collins here, that they would fail to secure a large audience for Mr. Jenkins on account of his lecture in my course in Boston, which, I was informed – had offended the 'mock loyalty,' as they phrased it, of the people of Montreal.

I leave the citizens of Montreal to decide whether, as a manager, I should have been justified in agreeing to disarrange the route of Mr. Collins to accommodate four or five imperious young lawyers who regard their debate as of greater public importance than the advent of a man whose books are now read by more persons who speak the English tongue than those of any other living author.

I ask them also to decide on the morality of these young men who, in the letter of one of their officers, now seek to create the impression that Mr. Collins is a 'failure;' and yet were willing to be responsible for what is ludicrously termed his '*intrusion*' into this city, if I had submitted to their arrogant conditions.

Yours truly, James Redpath[9]

The *Montreal Evening Star* responded to Redpath's 'Card' by stating that it 'fully resolves Mr Redpath from the imputations made'.

> With respect to the statement made by the President of the McGill Literary Society reflecting upon Mr. Redpath, Mr. Wilkie Collins' agent, a card is published this morning, which fully absolves Mr. Redpath from the imputations made. The root of this unpleasant muddle appears to have been a breach of faith in the part of the American Literary Bureau which led Mr. Collins to cancel all engagements made by it for him. That this should have led to disappointments, heart burnings and high words among parties in no way concerned with the original quarrel is not surprising. It is unfortunate that the Literary Society's debate takes place simultaneously with Mr. Collins' reading, but the insinuation that this was planned is absurd. An agent's desire is a clear field, not rival entertainments.
>
> On the score of attendance, we should be sorry to imagine that Montreal cannot supply crowded audiences for both debate and reading. The trouble is many persons would like to attend both. It is here that the uses of the 'blanket sheets' of the press become apparent, and we hope that our big contemporaries will dish up these twin literary treats in good style. We also hope that the Literary Society and Mr. Redpath will yet shake hands. This is not the season for quarrels. A misunderstanding seems to be at the bottom of the tiff; let matters be mutually explained calmly and dispassionately. The lesson taught is embodied in an old saying, and a true one, 'There is nothing certain except death and quarter-day.'[10]

The two events proceeded concurrently – and successfully – on the evening of 22 December. The University Society debated 'Ought the People of Canada to look forward to independence as their political future, rather than to a Federation of the Self-Governing Portions of the British Empire' at Association Hall, and Wilkie Collins read 'The Dream Woman: a Mystery' at Queen's Hall. Reviews the next morning reported an 'overflowing audience'[11] at the former and 'a large and influential audience amply filling the hall'[12] at the latter. A piece in the *Herald* concluded with the words:

> We are gratified that Mr. Collins has favored us with a visit and have no doubt that the visit will confirm in their admiration of his wonderful fictions, and in their expectancy of further works from his pen, those whom the celebrity of his name drew to the Queen's Hall last night.[13]

Toronto and Niagara Falls

On the morning after the reading, Collins, Frank Ward and James Redpath left for Toronto. The 'fifteen mortal hours of railway traveling', Collins wrote to Sebastian Schlesinger, was gruelling, made bearable only by

> a compartment to ourselves, a faithful and attentive nigger to wait on us, dry champagne, and a cold turkey.[14]

Collins expressed his pleasure with Toronto, describing the Rossin House Hotel,[15] on the corner of York and King Streets, as 'a good one' (Figure 8.1), and adding that Hunter, Rose, his publishers, were 'taking the greatest care of us'. He also wrote of his deep appreciation for his godson: 'Ward becomes more and more indispensable to my existence every day'.[16]

He and Ward were guests at the home of George Rose and his wife for Christmas Dinner. Collins's hosts apparently went out of their way to entertain him, even bundling him up and taking him for a ride in a sleigh. In spite of his usual hostility toward any festivities associated with the Christmas season, he later wrote to Rose that his visit to Toronto was 'one of the most agreeable visits in our travelling experience'.[17]

On 26 December, Boxing Day, Collins gave his dramatic reading of 'The Dream Woman' to a full house at the Music Hall under the auspices of the Directors of the Mechanics Institute. The *Leader* reported the following day that many had come to see 'an author so celebrated in the ranks of literature'. However, the reviewer observed that Collins's spectacles destroyed any attempt at facial expression and further lamented that he lacked 'all the elements that go

Figure 8.1: In Toronto, Collins stayed at the Rossin House Hotel, pronouncing it 'a good one' (Toronto Public Library (TRL): T 11075, with permission).

to constitute a good actor or a reasonably good reader', and although 'he told the story with all the grace and polish of a finished gentleman ... as a public reader he need never hope for success'.[18]

On Friday, 27 December, the Roses sent Collins and Ward on their way to Niagara, arranging for them to be met by a Mr Smeaton, who saw them through the Custom House at the border and served as their guide to the Falls.[19] Collins had been quite concerned about the visit, writing to Schlesinger from Toronto,

> My next duty is a severe one – Niagara. The lake here makes me feel rheumatic. What will the waterfall do? Besides, I don't like waterfalls – they are noisy.[20]

However, once he experienced the magnificence of Niagara, he enthusiastically wrote to Rose,

> No words can tell how these wonderful Falls astonished and impressed me. It is well worth the voyage from England to see Niagara alone.[21]

More Issues in Buffalo

While Collins and Ward were seeing the wonders of Niagara Falls, James Redpath had gone ahead to Buffalo, New York to make arrangements for a reading there.[22] Upon arrival, he discovered that the American Literary Bureau had scheduled Collins for an earlier reading of which he had been unaware, and thus failed to honour. Once again, Redpath was called upon to exercise his public relations expertise on Collins's behalf. He revealed the record of mismanagement by the American Literary Bureau to the Buffalo newspapers, resulting in a full disclosure in the *Courier.* The piece began with a tirade against bureaus in general, and then described the fraud and negligence associated with Collins's tour:

> LITERARY BUREAU MISMANAGEMENT – MR. WILKIE COLLINS
>
> There is no reason why the literary or lyceum bureau, so-called, should be other than a thoroughly useful institution, and yet it is certain that in the majority of cases it succeeds instead in making itself a public nuisance. On remote and helpless communities it annually inflicts a mass of oral trash in the shape of lectures by nameless humbugs, and when it undertakes to introduce to the public someone whom the pubic really desires to meet, the odds are numerous that it contrives to create, instead of a pleasant acquaintance, an inaccurate misunderstanding and mutual disgust. Complaints are constantly reaching us from lecturers victimized and lyceums befooled by the ingenious mismanagement or knavery of the bureau, and one by one the leading public speakers of the country are learning to dispense with its unlucky intervention altogether.
>
> An illustration of this vicious tendency to muddle things is furnished in the operations of a New York bureau as intermediary between Mr. Wilkie Collins and

the American public. Mr. Collins, before leaving England, authorized this concern to arrange ten preliminary appointments for readings in cities of this country. He came and met these, but while doing so, discovered, to his amazement, that the bureau had gone on and made engagements for him along the whole line of an extensive tour. This was done utterly without authority and on terms regarding which he had never been consulted. Of course he refused to be bound by such arrangements, whereupon the bureau cunningly set to work to throw upon him the odium of having broken a number of appointments of which he had known absolutely nothing. The engagement with the Buffalo Young Men's Association was one of these, and the false impression that Mr. Collins had capriciously thrown it up was conveyed at the instance of the bureau, to the minds of our disappointed lecture-goers. Nothing could have been more unfair, and we feel that we only do Mr. Collins the barest justice in stating the circumstances which furnish his complete vindication before the public. The fact that he has not sought any relief from the imputation of bad faith laid upon him should only, it seems to us, make the popular acceptance of this brief but ample explanation all the more prompt and hearty. The press in Cleveland and other cities west of us, which in this matter, by the ingenious perversity of the bureau, were put in the same boat as Buffalo, will doubtless take pleasure in correcting the consequent misapprehension which may possess the popular mind there as here.[23]

Problems with American lecture managers were far from unique to Collins's reading tour. The *Boston Commonwealth* printed an editorial expressing its frustration with the bureaus:

The Lecture Bureaus – We have had little to say lately concerning the inutility and expense of these institutions to lecture committees and lecturers alike; but it was not because there was no complaint of their partiality and mismanagement – rather because sometimes if an evil is let alone it will cure itself. The fault-finding of those who have been through the institutions grows louder month by month and year by year. Could some intelligent young man, with sufficient leisure, organize the dissatisfied patrons of these bureaus into a mutual protection association, there would be universal surprise at the extent and ramifications of the disappointment. We are assured by well-known lecturers and readers that they have done with the bureaus; by lecture-agents and committees that they shall make no further engagements through the bureaus. A widespread distrust prevails, and hard stories are told of the manner in which unwelcome lecturers are foisted upon committees and the public. We advise a conference of lecture-managers before another season to see if they cannot right this matter into something like the old-time mutuality of interest between speaker and committee, and on terms that will be creditable to both. At present the lecture system is in a languishing and unsatisfactory condition.[24]

The editorial clearly met a receptive audience because a week later a response appeared in the same newspaper:

Your article under the head of 'Minor Matters,' in your last issue, in regard to the humbug and abuse of the Lecture bureau system, meets with a warm response from your many readers who have suffered this incubus to remain so long upon our lyceums, and all kindred institutions, for the improvement of the people that it has become like the 'Old Man of the Sea around the neck of Sinbad,' clinging upon almost all literary effort of a public nature with the tenacity of a dying gladiator. This monopoly of lecturers has been as bad as any speculation of the Chicago grain-market, and as much effort has been put forth for a 'corner' on brains as ever characterized the operations in Wall Street over Erie, on any of the fancy stocks put forward by unscrupulous financiers on the brokers' board. No sooner has a popular lecturer landed on our shores than he is at once interviewed and secured by the 'Bureau,' and the larger the compensation the larger the commission; and we are told that some of these bureaus have charged as high as thirty-three per cent! Nay, even more; agents have crossed the Atlantic for the express purpose of looking up and securing gentlemen proposing to visit America, designing to enter upon a tour of lectures. The result has been that only the cities and more populous towns have been able to afford first-class talent, and at that have often been most egregiously taken in, getting no better lecture than could have been given by a score of their own townsmen, gratuitously, or for a nominal sum. As you truly say, Mr. Editor, the people have been patiently waiting to see if this evil would not cure itself, but your suggestion of a *conference of lecture committees* is such a commonsense remedy that I hope it will be tried.

A SUFFERER[25]

Collins and Ward arrived in Buffalo on 29 December and checked into the grand Tifft House Hotel. They were given the luxurious suite where Grand Duke Alexis of Russia had stayed during his visit in 1871. Collins's Buffalo reading was not scheduled until 6 January, giving him more than a week to relax and catch up with his correspondence, and to enjoy Buffalo's varied theatre offerings. In addition, he was invited to the Buffalo Club, founded by US President and city father Millard Fillmore in 1867. It was customary for the Club to welcome visiting dignitaries and provide them with up to a two-week membership. During the time of Collins's stay in Buffalo, the clubhouse was conveniently located near the hotel on the northwest corner of Delaware and Chippewa Streets.[26]

The evening of Collins's arrival, Redpath accompanied him to the Academy of Music to see Tommaso Salvini as Hamlet. The press spotted the two in a private box, applauding the famous Italian tragedian whom Collins had met earlier at the Lotos Club banquet in New York.[27] He also enjoyed a performance of Shelby's 'Comique', comprised of several black acts, female minstrels and athletic feats by the 'Monster Comique Company'.[28] The *Courier* reported that Collins was 'highly pleased with our theater', adding that he found it 'one of the most charming places of entertainment that he has visited in this country'.[29]

A few days later, Collins wrote a long and thoughtful letter to Frederick Lehmann, sharing his impressions of and experiences with the American people.[30]

Buffalo, New York

January 2, 1874

Strange to say, my dear Fred, I have actually got some leisure time at this place. A disengaged half-hour is before me, and I occupy it in writing a sort of duplicate letter for the Padrona[31] and for you.

I hear you have called, like a good fellow, at Gloucester Place, and have heard something of me there from time to time. No matter where I go my reception in America is always the same. The prominent people in each place visit me, drive me out, dine me, and do all that they can to make me feel myself among friends. The enthusiasm and the kindness are really and truly beyond description. I should be the most ungrateful man living if I had any other than the highest opinion of the American people. I find them to be the most enthusiastic, the most cordial, and the most sincere people I have ever met with in my life. When an American says, 'Come and see me,' he <u>means</u> it. This is wonderful to an Englishman.

Before I had been a week in this country I noted three national peculiarities which had never been mentioned to me by visitors to ~~this country~~ the 'States.' I. No American hums or whistles a tune – either at home or in the street. II. Not one American in 500 has a dog. III. Not one American in a 1000 carries a walking stick. I, who hum perpetually – who love dogs – who cannot live without a walking stick – am greatly distressed at finding my dear Americans deficient in the three social virtues just enumerated.

My readings have succeeded by surprising the audiences. The story surprises them in the first place – being something the like of which they have not heard before. And my way of reading surprises them in the second place – because I don't flourish a paper-knife, and stamp about the platform, and thump the reading desk. I persist in keeping myself in the [*long cross-out*] background and the story in front. The audience begins at each reading with silent astonishment, and ends with a great burst of applause.

As to the money, if I could read often enough, I should bring back a little fortune – in spite of the panic. The hard times have been against me of course – but while others have suffered badly, I have always drawn audiences. Here, for example, they give me a fee for reading on Tuesday evening next – it amounts to between 70 pounds and 80 pounds (English). If I could read five time a week at this rate (which is my customary rate) here is 350 pounds a week – which is not bad pay for an hour and three-quarters' reading each night. But I cannot read five times a week without knocking myself up – [*erased*] and this I won't do. And then I have been mismanaged and cheated by my agents – have had to change them, and start afresh with a new man. The result had been loss of time, and loss of money. But I am <u>investing</u> in spite of it – and (barring accidents) I am a fair way to make far more than I have made yet, before the last fortnight in March – when I propose to sail for home. I am going 'out West' from this – and I <u>may</u> get as far as the Mormons. My new agent – a first-rate man – is ahead making engagements; and I am here (thanks to the kindness of Sebastian Schlesinger) with my godson Frank as secretary and companion. I find him a perfect treasure – I don't know what I should do without him.

As for the said Sebastian S. he is the brightest nicest kindest little fellow I have met with for many a long day. He wouldn't hear of my dining at the Hotel while I was in Boston this last time. Whenever I had no engagement (and I kept out of engagements, having work to do) I dined at his house – and dined superbly. *Mrs. S had just lain in of a daughter – so I have still to be presented to her – and our dinners were of the bachelor sort.* [*erased*] It is not one of the least of Sebastian's virtues that he speaks with the greatest affection of <u>you</u>. He also makes the best cocktail in America. Vive Sebastian.

Barthold S. was also as kind as could be. I dined with him too in New York. So you see your letters have not been thrown away.

The nigger-waiters (I like them better than the American waiters) are ringing the dinner bell. I must go and feed off a variety of badly cooked meats and vegetables ranged around me in (say) soap dishes. Otherwise, I am comfortable here. I have got the Russian Grand Duke's bedroom – and [*erased*] a parlour in which I can shake hands with my visitors – and a box at the theatre – and the freedom of the Club.

Write soon, my dear boy, and tell me about yourself and the Padrona – to whom I send my best love and sincerest good wishes. She is happily settled, I hope, in the new house. I want to hear all about the new house – and about the boys – God forgive me! I am [*erased*] writing of Rudy as if he was a boy. Don't tell him! The fact is I am getting to be an old man – I shall be fifty if I live till the 8th of this month – and I shall celebrate my birthday by giving a reading at 'Cleveland.' I wish I could transport myself to London!

Yours my dear Fred always, Afftly
Wilkie Collins

Collins also wrote that morning to both his American and his Canadian publishers. He told Joseph Harper of his misadventures with his managers and shared with Hunter, Rose his views concerning Canadian copyright legislation to determine set publication fees.[32]

On 3 January, while Collins was in Buffalo, *Man and Wife*, the third of his plays to open during his visit, made its second American run at the Fifth Avenue Theater in New York City, the first having been three years earlier. The female lead was played by Ada Dyas, who had played Marian Halcombe in the London production of *The Woman in White*.[33]

On Friday afternoon, Collins joined a number of prominent Buffalo citizens for an excursion to the Farrar & Trefts Machine Works on Perry Street. The group was treated to a tour of a self-propelled torpedo boat invented by Buffalo native John Lay. Mr Lay and his superintendent, Mr M. Hubbee, allowed their visitors a critical examination of the various parts and explained the inner workings of this 'consummate engine of destruction'. In declining to attempt a description of the excruciating process of bringing the torpedo from concept to maturity, the *Courier* said that 'it would require the subtle and vigorous pen of Wilkie Collins to write it, and so we leave the matter to others than ourself for fitting treatment'.[34]

Collins's Buffalo reading was given on Tuesday, 6 January 1874 at St James Hall, as part of the Young Men's Association lecture course. Admission to the event was $0.50.[35] Although the weather was 'unpropitious,' the house was crowded (Figure 8.2), the papers admitting that

> Doubtless half the members of his audience ... attended the reading mainly for the purpose of seeing one of their favorite authors *in propria persona* ... Had the Dream Woman been written and read by an unknown author, it would have excited but little interest.[36]

Figure 8.2: A view from the audience in an auditorium where Collins would typically speak from behind a cloth-covered table on the stage (Buffalo and Erie County Historical Society, with permission).

9 THE FINAL CIRCUIT: CLEVELAND, DETROIT AND CHICAGO

From Buffalo, Collins continued west along the southern shore of Lake Erie[1] to Cleveland, Ohio, arriving on 8 January, his fiftieth birthday. The press announcements for his reading that evening spoke to his attraction as 'one whose creations pass into the common speech and thought of mankind' causing 'a desire as universal and as old as the world' to see what manner of man he was.[2] The reading was to be at Case Hall, on the corner of Superior and East Third Streets, and locally considered the most noted concert hall of its day. The third-floor auditorium accommodated 2,000 people in what were then called 'patent opera chairs'. Its walls and ceilings, decorated by Italian artist Garibaldi, had echoed the voices of Bret Harte, Mark Twain, Horace Greeley, and Henry Ward Beecher. Reserved seats for Collins's reading were available for \$0.75 and \$1.00.[3] The evening began at 'precisely eight o'clock [when] Mr. Collins stepped down upon the platform with a firm, quick step, unattended by the usual "introducer"'.[4] Throughout the performance, the audience listened with 'intense interest', and not one person left the hall early.

On the following evening, Collins was in nearby Sandusky, Ohio where he gave a reading to 'a very fair audience' at the Opera House.[5] E. S. Payson, who, under Redpath's auspices had assisted with Dickens's visit, had come ahead to firm up the arrangements and met Collins on his arrival.[6] The next day's review was positive, stating that Collins's reading was 'well rendered and was listened to with rapt attention'.[7] That night, Collins and Ward stayed at the Lake House Hotel, where he wrote to George Bentley, 'the snow is falling and the Lake is close under my windows'.[8]

Continuing west along the lake for sixty miles to Toledo, Ohio, Collins gave a reading at the Wheeler Opera House on Monday evening, 12 January.[9] The review in the *Toledo Blade* described the 'paucity' of the audience and contained a lackluster response to the reading. It concluded:

> However bright the light of genius may shine in one direction, in another it may be entirely hidden from view.[10]

Proceeding north for another sixty miles, Collins arrived in Detroit, Michigan on 13 January for a reading that evening at the Opera House. Indicators of a successful performance were inauspicious: advertisements for the reading in two newspapers contained the wrong date,[11] and a newspaper commentary on the day of his appearance read:

> Ten seats are reserved for Sothern[12] where one is taken for the Wilkie Collins reading tonight. While the former will certainly have crowded houses, the latter will suffer the chagrin of learning that his reputation as a reader has preceded him.[13]

The reading, however, went well. The assembled group, in spite of a snowstorm, was 'larger than the average gatherings for entertainments of that character' and 'made up from our best society'. Collins met 'a warm reception' by the audience and was given their 'close attention',[14] thus assuring his satisfaction in spite of predictions.

Chicago

A gruelling overnight railroad journey brought Collins and Ward from Detroit to Chicago, Illinois, where they arrived on the morning of 16 January. They settled into the newly opened Sherman Hotel, located on the southwest corner of Randolph and Clark Streets. Designed by prominent Chicago architect William Boyington, it was considered one of the finest hotels in the city, catering to public figures in the stock and agricultural trade. Collins had little time to recuperate from the trip as his reading was scheduled for the evening of their arrival at the grand new Music Hall, located opposite the Sherman House on Clark Street.[15]

It could be expected that the people of Chicago would be out in great numbers to see the man who was 'widely known in the world of literature as a novelist of wonderful imagination'.[16] Both *Man and Wife* and *The New Magdalen* had recently run in the city, the former at Hooley's Theater, with Augustin Daly's Fifth Avenue Company[17] and the latter at the Academy of Music, starring Carlotta Leclercq.[18]

For Collins's reading of 'The Dream Woman', the *Chicago Tribune* estimated that the hall's 1,700 seats were only about half filled, albeit with 'an unusual number of local celebrities, the church being unusually well represented'. Among these was Robert Collyer, popular pastor of Unity Church and founding member and first president of the Chicago Literary Club. Others in the audience included Rev. W. H. Thomas, Rev. H. N. Powers, Rev. Edward Sullivan and Rev. Clinton Locke, as well as the City Sealer.[19]

The *Tribune* mentioned that the hall was uncomfortably cold in spite of its new steam heating system,[20] and reported 'the calorific apparatus of the hall stupendously defective'.[21] The *Chicago Evening Journal* suggested, 'Perhaps the frigidity of the atmosphere had something to do with the rigidity of the audience'. The reviews were not complimentary. The *Journal*'s response, although unique in observation, was not unlike the others in tone:

> But not withstanding the reader's monotonous cockney accent and jerky elocution and inability to change from his own tone to the imaginary ones of his characters, the reading was worth all it cost to anybody simply because it was done by one of the great masters of English fiction.[22]

Apparently, the arduous rail journey to Chicago had caused Collins to reassess his travel plans. In Buffalo, early in January, he was still considering his western adventure, writing to Fred Lehmann, 'I am going 'Out West'... and I may get as far as the Mormons'.[23] At one point he had even considered continuing as far as the Pacific coast.[24] He had cousins, relatives of his mother, who lived in San Francisco, whom he had hoped to see. [25] On 9 January, he was still considering travelling some distance west. He wrote to George Bentley from Sandusky that he was 'on [his] way to Chicago and the Western towns'.[26] But after arriving in Chicago, Collins's attitude seemed to change. He wrote to Joseph Harper, 'My plans are a little uncertain'.[27] He was more forthcoming in writing to Jane Bigelow, admitting,

> I am not going further West, because I cannot endure the railway traveling. A night in a 'sleeping car' destroys me for days afterwards.[28]

In Jane, Collins sensed a sympathetic ear, and he shared with her his impressions of the brash new city that had not only emerged from a frontier settlement in less than fifty years, but from the ashes of the Great Fire[29] two years earlier. Calling Chicago 'this city of magnificent warehouses', he continued:

> Don't tell anybody – but the truth is I am not sorry to leave Chicago. The dull sameness of the great blocks of iron and brick overwhelms me. The whole city seems to be saying 'See how rich I am after the fire, and what a tremendous business I do!' and everybody I meet uses the same form of greeting. 'Two years ago, Mr. Collins, this place was a heap of ruins – are you not astonished when you see it now?' I am not a bit astonished. It is a mere question of raising money – the re-building follows as a matter of course.[30]

This letter reflects a significant reversal of attitude. Shortly after the Fire, Collins had sent a check for five pounds[31] to the Committee of the American Chicago Relief Fund, along with the following heartfelt message:

90 Gloucester Place
Portman Square W.

31st October 1871
Gentlemen,

I beg to enclose a cheque for Five pounds, offered to your Fund, as a trifling expression of my sympathy with the sufferers by the Fire of Chicago, and of my sincere admiration of the heroic spirit with which your countrymen have met the disaster that has fallen on them.

I remain, Gentlemen,
Your obedient servant,
Wilkie Collins[32]

Collins's apparent disaffection with Chicago was probably because of his weariness, travel schedule and extended absence from home. Distances within the United States were great, and the trains were jolting and often overheated. In spite of the reduced number of his readings, his schedule remained exhausting. In a letter to Schlesinger on 17 January he mentioned his altered plans, adding that he would explain it all when they next met. He and Ward would start back to Boston after the weekend, breaking the journey in Detroit and Rochester. He again wrote of his aversion to rail travel:

> On the way here, I tried the 'sleeping car' – and lay wide-awake ... all night. Nothing will induce me to repeat the experiment. I feel the 'sleeping car' in the 'small of my back' and on the drums of my ears, at this moment.[33]

10 ARGUMENTS AND ACCOLADES: RETURN TO NEW ENGLAND

Collins and Ward left Chicago on Monday, 19 January as planned, stopping for the night in Detroit, where they stayed at the Russell House Hotel. The *Detroit Evening News* happily reported that Collins 'wanted to see more of Detroit'.[1] More probably he wished to avoid another night on the train.

By Thursday, 22 January, they were back in Boston, but did not return to the Tremont Hotel. Instead they chose the St James, perhaps after coming to the same conclusion that Dickens did on his return to the US when he wrote to his subeditor that the Tremont had 'become contemptible'.[2]

Concerns at home of both a business and personal nature directed Collins's attention toward London, necessitating his writing to his solicitor, William Tindell about an unsanctioned revival of *The New Magdalen* at an unsuitable venue, and a problem with the lease on the home he shared with Martha Rudd. He also, for the first time, suggested that the financial panic was having an effect on his audiences.[3]

However, by 28 January, Collins seemed to have regained his energy. Writing to Schlesinger, he good-naturedly blamed his manager for failing to tell him about a reading in Salem, Massachusetts, and accepted an invitation to dine with his friend on Saturday.[4]

Collins read to a full house at the Essex Institute in Salem on Friday, 30 January, as part of the Institute Course. The reading began at 7.15 so that he might catch the train back to Boston afterwards.[5] The reports once again asserted that as a novelist he was second to none, but as a reader, 'the least said about him, the better'.[6]

At 2.00 the following afternoon, Collins made his second Boston appearance,[7] this time at the Tremont Temple, a large hall used on Sundays by the Union Temple Church. The audience was 'satisfactory in both numbers and appreciation'. The review made special mention of 'the charm of the reader's delivery' and called the entertainment 'in every respect a success' which must have proven 'very satisfactory to its leading spirit'.[8] Later, Redpath sent him a check for $12.81 for his share of the proceeds.[9]

Because he had already read 'The Dream Woman' on two occasions in Boston, Collins was urged by friends to give 'special attention' to his third and last reading there. Having no time to write something new, he set about preparing a novelized version of his early play *The Frozen Deep*, a story of heroism and self-sacrifice in the Artic. If he adapted *The Frozen Deep* with the same process that Dickens used in preparing his own works for an evening's reading, he would have abbreviated the work by combining summaries of various sections with bridge passages where cuts had been made, altering words and phrases for simplicity, and deleting characters and scenes not essential to the central plot.[10] He hastily wrote to Joseph Harper that he was so busy with it that it was 'not easy for me to give my mind to anything else'.[11]

During the first week of February, Collins made a short tour of New England, stopping first in Springfield, Massachusetts, where he read 'The Dream Woman' at the Opera House on the evening of 5 February. The review in the *Republican* suggested that if the audience 'did not have any expectation of such an entertainment as Charles Dickens' then Collins's reading would have left them well pleased.[12] He spent that night at the Haynes Hotel, leaving the following afternoon for Worcester, Massachusetts where he was scheduled to read under 'independent auspices',[13] with no local sponsorship.

The Worcester Controversy

Although Collins left Springfield at 1.30 for the fifty-mile trip to Worcester, a railroad accident near Warren delayed his arrival in town until 7.20, ten minutes before his scheduled appearance at Mechanics Hall.[14] This delay, however, was only the beginning of his problems. As he was hurrying to his waiting audience, he discovered for the first time that he had been scheduled to read there in November. Without Collins's knowledge or consent, the American Literary Bureau had made arrangements for him to appear in the local Anglo-American Lecture Course.

Collins's dismay can only be imagined, as he stepped up on the platform, breathless and agitated, and gave the following apology:

> I owe the people of Worcester two explanations, first for being late this evening, which is due to an accident on the railroad. The second is much more serious. I have now for the first time learned that I was advertised to appear here last November or December, and that the reason given for my non-appearance was that 'Wilkie Collins was sick'. Now, ladies and gentlemen, I assure you upon my honor that this whole transaction came about without my knowledge or consent. I have always been received in this country with the greatest courtesy and consideration and I could not show such marked disrespect to an American audience as this course would indicate. The whole thing was done by the American Lecture Bureau out of revenge for my having withdrawn my business from their hands.[15]

The local newspapers all carried the essence of Collins's apology to the people of Worcester. Reviews of his reading of 'The Dream Woman' were mixed. The *Daily Press* called it 'a weird sort of story' that was 'gradually seen to have no explanation whatever' but maintained, 'the dramatic force of the reader was enough to hold the attention of his auditors with a grasp of iron to the close'.[16] The *Gazette* applauded 'his intricate plot and the circumstantial ingenuity with which he convinces his readers that he is telling actual facts' but called the story 'repulsive ... even approach[ing] coarseness'.[17]

Collins returned to Boston on Sunday.[18] The extent of his celebrity had not abated, and he was forced to move to a third hotel, the Vendome on Commonwealth Avenue, to escape the relentless pursuit of autograph hunters.[19] On Monday, he received a letter from Redpath. Along with a check for Collins's share of the proceeds from the Boston afternoon reading, Redpath enclosed a clipping from the *Worcester Spy* on the issue of Collins's earlier failure to appear there. Appearing in the *Spy* on the front-page centre, and again in the *Worcester Evening Gazette* (with an introductory commentary) was the following article about Collins and Rev. William Parry,[20] manager of the Anglo-American Lecture Course in Worcester:

PARRY VS. COLLINS

Rev. Mr. Parry Rises to Explain

As our readers know, the explanation of Mr. Wilkie Collins on Friday night, in regard to his previous failure to appear, reflected on the American Literary Bureau, but certainly not directly on Rev. Mr. Parry, the manager of the ill-starred Anglo-American course. Mr. Parry nevertheless feels aggrieved, and desires to make an explanation. His absence at Southbridge prevented his making any reply on Saturday, but he returned towards evening, and wrote the following statement, which first appeared in this morning's *Spy*.

MR. PARRY'S CARD

I am, I think, the most unfortunate of mortals. I must be brother or next of kin to the man of the gospel who fell among thieves. Arriving in Worcester, Saturday, 5 ½ P.M., I read the astounding statement that Mr. Collins said he was never engaged to read in my course, in Worcester, and that he was not sick and on that account unable to appear, knowing nothing of the engagement. I must not run into temptation, and being unable to trust myself if I ventured to give the right names to such proceedings, I will present only bare facts and documents, leaving your readers to form their own opinions, and christen these 'ways that are dark' for themselves.

Wilkie Collins was engaged to read in the A.A.L.C. [Anglo-American Lecture Course] so far back as July 1873. The American Literary Bureau, through whom I engaged him, were then his exclusive agents. He was to have opened the course, October 3rd, but afterwards, the date was changed to November 14th. Here is Mr. Williams's letter:

American Literary Bureau
114 Washington Street, Boston
September 18, 1873

Rev. Wm. M. Parry, Dear Sir:

Your dates now stand Bret Harte, Dec. 2nd, Wilkie Collins, Nov. 14th, Prof. Pepper, Oct. 3d and 14th; Newman Hall, Dec. 12th; Temple Quartette, Nov. 24th. I did not intend to charge you so much for Pepper the second time. His price Oct. 3rd is $300 and Oct. 14th $200. Yours truly,

B.W. Williams

PS Newman Hall's subject shall be 'Prayer.'

I copy this letter verbatim. The letter is dated two months before the time when Mr. Collins was to appear.

In taking a long journey from home I called en route upon Mr. Williams that I might make sure Mr. Collins would appear. This was about seven days before Nov. 14th. Mr. Williams said Mr. Collins would appear: and a telegram was sent from the Bureau to the printers in Worcester announcing what Mr. Collins would read. The bills were printed accordingly. I returned home, arriving in Worcester at noon of Nov. 14, the day when Mr. Collins was to appear. The following telegrams were awaiting me, which I immediately made public.

(1.)

Boston, Nov. 10th, 1873
To Rev. Mr. Parry,
Wilkie Collins' health fails and probably cannot be at Worcester.
B.W. Williams

(2.)

Boston, Nov. 11th, 1873
To Rev. Mr. Parry,
Collins cannot read Friday night. B.W. Williams

Many of your readers will remember that Mr. Williams came to Worcester to see what could be done to appease the dissatisfied public, and upon his and others' representation that Bradlaugh would satisfy the public, that lecturer was engaged. To show the public I wished to treat them fairly, I added, without extra charge, the glee club concert that cost over $400, another lecturer, Miss Edgarton, and another Temple Quartette concert. The result is I have lost money. And now appears the amazing statement that Mr. Collins knew nothing about his engagement! All my lectures were engaged upon the distinct understanding that they were not to appear again in Worcester without my consent. This is always done, so I understand. Fancy my surprise when I read the recent announcement of Mr. Collins' s appearance in this city! I held it a breach of faith, and at once telegraphed the bureau demanding the reason why, without my consent, he was about to read here. Here is Mr. Williams's reply:

Boston, January 31, 1874
To Rev. Wm. M. Parry:
Have nothing to do with Collins now. Redpath runs him.
B.W. Williams

I have now told the public all that I know; that is, all that I can prove by documents. I have heard a rumor about some unpleasantness between Mr. Collins and the bureau, but as I have no proofs I will not repeat what may or may not be a simple rumor. It is lucky for me that I have the slovenly habit, which Lord Byron also contracted – that of never taking the trouble to burn letters or telegrams, and have thus been able to produce the above proofs. These documents I enclose that you may see them yourself and show them to anyone who desires to see them. You will kindly preserve them as I shall wish to have them returned. Now what am I to say about such proceedings? With whom lies the blame, Wilkie Collins or the bureau? I must forbear to put such questions lest I be tempted to attempt their answer. All I can say is that I consider myself about the best ill-used man in Worcester or out of it. Let me add, *until proof is produced, I will not believe that Mr. Collins would either privately or publicly state what he knew to be false;*[21] and that I have no proof that he is at all to blame in the matter. It will not be out of place for me to say in conclusion that I intended telling the public that Mr. Collins, according to my engagement with the bureau, had no right to read here without my consent, and also I intended publishing Mr. Williams' telegram in reply to my remonstrance. Why did I not do this before Mr. Collins appeared? For this simple reason, that I felt that, though I had been injured, I had no right to do anything calculated to prevent any one going to hear Mr. Collins. Had I been in town I should have been present on Friday evening, and no doubt Mr. Collins would have allowed me then to state in reply to his remarks what I now make public. It struck me that if I published Mr. Williams' reply to my remonstrance, after Mr. Collins had read, it would suit my purpose just as well, and could not then, of course, do any damage to his audience. Though I have lost considerable, and though the lecture bureau has not indemnified me to the amount of a single cent for the losses consequent upon Mr. Collins' and Bret Harte's non-appearance at the time advertised, I do not appeal to anyone for sympathy. All I ask of any man who does business with me is that he will strictly observe the business rules laid down in the ten commandments, and then I am perfectly satisfied. I do think, however, that Mr. Collins and Mr. Williams should settle this matter between themselves, so that the people of Worcester may know who is to blame. There is evidently a screw loose somewhere. What can Mr. Williams' laconic, and to me unsatisfactory reply import – 'Have nothing to do with Collins now; Redpath runs him?' Theirs is the misunderstanding; mine is the loss. Let me close my letter with the first sentence I wrote in the first A.A.L.C. controversy – 'I never deceive the public.'

I am, yours truly,
Wm. M. Parry[22]

Collins responded to Redpath on 10 February:

Hotel Vendome
W. Boston
10th Feby 1874

Dear Mr. Redpath,

Thanks for a cheque for $12.81 – due to me on the proceeds of the Boston afternoon reading.

I am obliged to you for the newspaper slip. I will consider the propriety of writing a reply – but it seems to <u>me</u> that the matter lies between Mr. Williams and Mr. Parry. Mr. Parry expressly says, 'Until proof is produced I will not believe that Mr. Collins would either publicly or privately state what he knew to be false.' The best way I think will be for me to write personally to Mr. Parry, on the subject.

Vy truly yours,
Wilkie Collins[23]

It is not known if Collins wrote to Rev. Parry, but perhaps he decided that enough had been said on the matter already. Besides, he was back in Boston with friends, and busy with preparations for his new reading.

In addition to comfortable evenings with Sebastian Schlesinger, he was frequently invited to dine with members of Boston society, including James and Annie Fields and Charles F. Morse, a Civil War hero.[24]

An Extraordinary Evening

On 16 February, Collins was honoured by 'a select group of his most intimate friends'[25] at a banquet at the St James Hotel. Organized by Boston publisher William Gill, the remarkable assembly included Henry Wadsworth Longfellow, John Greenleaf Whittier, Oliver Wendell Holmes and Samuel Langhorne Clemens (Mark Twain), as well as Josiah Quincy (one-time mayor of Boston), Thomas Wentworth Higginson (theologian and author), Edwin Percy Whipple (essayist and critic) and the Vice-President of the United States, Henry Wilson.[26]

The company first met for formal introductions in a private parlour before adjourning to dinner 'in one of the cozy little dining rooms to be found at the St. James'.[27] The banquet table was richly decorated with greenhouse flowers and a 'select orchestra' played selections from Strauss, Verdi, and Beinecke in the background.[28] Dinner consisted of twelve courses, and included such delicacies as cod's tongues a la tartar, larded quail and stuffed mongrel goose.[29] Over brandy, Joseph Quincy

> proposed the health of their distinguished visitor, who rose to his feet and made a short and very delicate little speech, expressing his satisfaction at his reception in this country and the warm friends whom he had met and whom he should always regard with high esteem. Colonel Higginson followed in a few words appropriate to the occasion, and Mark Twain gave a brief description of his reception in England, saying he thought he was very successful in the object of his visit there, which was to teach the people good morals, and to introduce some of the improvements of the present century.

Edwin Whipple then made a speech that must have been particularly gratifying to Collins. It captured not only the magic of his art as a writer, but touched on fair copyright laws on both sides of the ocean, an issue particularly important to him.

Mr. Chairman – We are all glad to meet the distinguished guest of the evening, and we are sorry that he is so soon to leave us. We were all familiar with the offspring of his brain long before we met the father of the numerous family, now inhabiting that region of imagination which he has colonized, namely, Collins's Land. It is the peculiar characteristic of this eminent writer that he has given to his romances an air of matter of fact. One would as soon doubt of the reality and veracity of Robinson Crusoe as of some of the beings he has created. Indeed, I doubt not that you, as well as the rest of us, have often sacrificed an hour or two, when practical business most pressed on your time, to read the new monthly number of one of his serial novels. The art of stimulating – and puzzling curiosity, of cunningly postponing the explanation of the mystery, he seems continually on the point of explaining, in not only holding the attention of the reader, but exasperating it, there rarely has been a more delightfully provoking inventor of plots than the gentleman whom we have the pleasure now to meet. We, of course, all feel vexed that he is going away. We should like to naturalize him – to make him a fellow citizen, not merely of the Republic of Letters, but of the Republic of the United States. Perhaps we might succeed in doing it were it not that the reality of his characters is ten times more clear and strong to him than it is to us. He is called home by the 'Woman in White,' and 'Poor Miss Finch,' and the lady who has 'No Name,' who all say that they cannot live without him. Then his brother Brahmin novelists in England – he, you know, belongs to highest 'Caste' – are ravenous to get back to their 'Moonstone,' which we, they think, have filched. Well, we must let him go, though we hope he will steal a six months' vacation here and there, to visit us again – and again. When he gets back to England we feel sure he will not reverse the point of the famous couplet, in speaking of his American brothers, in brain and blood, if not brothers-in-law. He will not say –

Be to their faults a little kind,
Be to their virtues very blind.

He will carry back to his native land a firm feeling and conviction that he is as welcome here as he is honored in England – that the intellectual community of the two nations is thoroughly socialistic; that all intelligent and conscientious readers of books are as anxious that his copyrights should be as much respected in New York without law as they are in London with law, and that we hope soon to give to him, and to all his brother authors in England, a legal sanction to what is now merely a compromise between publishers.

After the speeches, Oliver Wendell Holmes read a poem that he had written especially for the occasion:

A Toast to Wilkie Collins

The painter's and the poet's fame
Shed their twinned luster round his name,
To gild our story-teller's art,
Where each in turn must play his part.

What scenes from Wilkie's pencil sprung,
The minstrel saw but left unsung!
What shapes the pen of Collins drew,
No painter clad in living hue!

But on our artist's shadowy screen
A stranger miracle is seen
Than priest unveils or pilgrim seeks –
The poem breathes, the picture speaks!

And so his double name comes true,
They christened better than they knew,
And Art proclaims him twice her son –
Painter and poet, both in one![30]

At the close of the evening, each guest was presented with a bon-bon box, in the shape and size of the Cabinet edition of Collins's works, covered in Turkish leather, and containing his photograph, his autograph and 'the number of his important works exactly corresponding with the number present at the reception'.[31]

Collins must have still been feeling euphoric when he wrote to Schlesinger, 'Such a banquet yesterday!' adding that the only detail the papers failed to mention was 'a dove with a pen in her mouth – hanging from the chandelier'.[32]

11 WINDING DOWN: NEW YORK AND WALLINGFORD

The days in Boston continued to be pleasant ones. Collins dined with the Schlesingers often[1] and visited other American friends. However, his correspondence began to reveal that his thoughts were turning to his family and friends in London. He was weary and ready to go home. Although he had originally planned to remain in the United States until the end of March, he wrote to his old friend, Charles Ward,

> I have decided on returning by the boat which leaves this port on the 7th of March. The Times are bad. There is nothing very profitable to be done – and I want to be home again.[2]

Collins accepted a copy of a collection of short stories by Boston novelist John Trowbridge, which he promised he would read on the voyage home, and which he kept in his library for the rest of his life.[3] On Friday, 21 February, he dined with Henry Wadsworth Longfellow at Craigie House in Cambridge. A few days later, Longfellow wrote to his sister-in-law, Mary Appleton Mackintosh:

> We are thriving here in the Craigie House, in our usual quiet way. We see most of the English who pass this way – have had Wilkie Collins at dinner ...[4]

Collins gave a farewell performance for 'his friends and admirers in Boston' on Friday, 27 February.[5] This time the reading was at Parker Memorial Hall, a smaller venue with 850 seats on the corner of Berkeley and Appleton Streets. He read his newly reworked version of *The Frozen Deep*. As a benefit to the people of Boston, tickets were only $0.50.[6] Although the 'fine audience' was held in 'close attention', the *Boston Daily Globe* noted that Collins's theme had been plagiarized and recently dramatized at a city theatre production called 'Polaris'. When interviewed, Collins sarcastically responded 'that though American laws protected his watch and his pocket-book, they did not throw their sheltering arms around the product of his brain'. The review concluded, however, that the reading was 'very good, better, perhaps than any of his previous ones in this city'.[7]

On Saturday morning, 28 February, Collins accompanied publisher William Gill to the Saturday Club,[8] a small group of distinguished friends who met at the Parker House Hotel on the last Saturday afternoon of every month to read poetry and discuss literary matters. Among the great moments in the Club's history was Dickens's first American reading of *A Christmas Carol*. At the gathering, Collins was able to again visit with some of the men who had shared in his special evening at the St. James, including John Whittier, Oliver Holmes and Henry Longfellow.[9]

On 1 March, Collins returned for the last time to his quarters at the Westminster Hotel in New York.[10] Once settled, he wrote a series of letters arranging to visit friends and attending to business before his departure. He informed Joseph Harper that he would come by Franklin Square on Tuesday morning in order to congratulate him on his 'dissolution of partnership with R.G. [rheumatic gout]'.[11] He also made arrangements to visit Jane Bigelow at her West 25th Street home in the afternoon.[12] In a hurried note dashed off to William Tindell that same day, he sent particulars of his life insurance policies 'in case I am drowned', adding 'the room [is] full of people'.[13]

During those hectic two days, journalists, acquaintances and admirers came to wish him farewell. George Butler, a journalist with *Wilkes' Spirit of the Times*, paid his respects, as did Shakespearian actor John McCullough.[14] Collins may also have visited with fellow Englishman Edward Sothern, who was staying at the Gramercy Park Hotel,[15] or John Latrobe, his host in Baltimore, who had checked into the Fifth Avenue Hotel on the same day as Collins's return to the city.[16] Collins also managed a final dinner with Albert Fechter and two or three other friends.[17]

A Visit to the Wallingford Perfectionists

On the morning of 4 March, in the midst of his New York farewells, Collins slipped away on a brief expedition to the Wallingford Community of Perfectionists in Connecticut.[18] William Gill arranged the trip.[19] Apparently, Collins had been interested in visiting the Oneida Community in New York, a 'free love' society founded in 1848 by the eccentric genius John Henry Noyes.[20] However, he had been unable to determine its location and fit it into his schedule. Perhaps Collins had shared his disappointment at not being able to tour the community with Gill when they were attending the Saturday Club meeting, for Gill contacted a branch of the Oneida Community in nearby Wallingford and made arrangements for Collins to visit the following Wednesday.

Wallingford was a smaller offshoot of the Oneida Community of Perfectionists that, in 1874, consisted of about forty-five members. Founded in 1851, it occupied 366 acres, including a small lake. The community in Wallingford upheld the same beliefs as its mother centre at Oneida: that the Bible was the 'text-book of the Spirit of truth', that the Gospel provided for total salvation from sin, and that a complete community of goods and persons was commanded by Jesus. That last principle was what justified the extraordinary social system in which there was no marriage, or rather instead, a 'complex marriage'. The ideal of 'complex marriage', in the practice of the Perfectionists, meant that any man and any woman within the community, with the consent of the leadership, might cohabit, as long as there was no 'exclusive and idolatrous attachment'.[21]

Collins and Ward took the Hartford train and were joined by a reporter from the *New Haven Register* before they arrived in Wallingford at noon.[22] During the half hour that the reporter had with Collins on the train, he made the following observations:

> [Collins] is well pleased with this country, and remarked that the climate was very agreeable to him, also that the people had been very kind and his journeys had been exceedingly pleasant. Of the hotels in America, he said that they were magnificent, and were especially deserving of credit for their good beds, which were always well aired and very clean and comfortable. Of the tables, he remarked that an abundant supply was always at hand, but the enormous variety of vegetables, side dishes, etc., were so numerous, that it was almost impossible to taste of one before the other was getting too cold to be palatable. His general conceptions of the habits of the country were generally favorable and in the main correct.[23]

Collins and Ward received a warm reception at the Community, whose members expressed their 'gratification in receiving so distinguished a guest' although his visit 'rippled ... the usually tranquil surface of our quiet life'.[24] During his three-hour visit, Collins was treated to dinner and a tour of the grounds. Charles Joslyn, superintendent of the printing operation, a music teacher, and a lawyer for the Community,[25] served as guide. Collins was shown the Town Hall, selectmen's room, town clerk's office, and the Episcopal Church, which he remarked 'was the finest structure of the kind that he had seen in the country'.[26] At the printing office (Figure 11.1), Joslyn showed Collins some photographs and past copies of the *Oneida Circular* and presented him with a set of stereographs of the Community. The *Circular* gave a detailed report of the interview Collins had granted to Community members:

> Mr. Collins had, as he informed us, been anxious to visit the Community during his stay in America, but was unable to find anyone who could inform him of the whereabouts of 'Oneida Creek'[27] and so had hitherto been unable to localize us. He regretted that his limited time in this county would not permit him to visit Oneida, but promises to return again in a year or two, when he will devote a part of his time to the O. C.
>
> Mr. Collins is a genial, modest gentleman fifty years of age, whose countenance you are doubtless familiar with from his portrait. He speaks highly of the hospitality

Figure 11.1: The Printing House at the Wallingford Oneida Community, where Superintendent Charles Joslyn gave Collins a tour of the Community's printing operation (Oneida Collection, Syracuse University, with permission).

with which he has everywhere been received in America, and seems pleased with his popularity as an author, though he is quite backward in speaking of his own productions, and evidently prefers other topics of conversation. He was an intimate friend of Dickens, and on several occasions the two wrote a short story together, forming a sort of literary co-partnership not unusual among authors.

'On one of these occasions,' said Mr. Collins, 'we agreed to exchange styles, so as to puzzle the critics; Mr. Dickens was to adopt my style, and I was to imitate his. The plan succeeded perfectly, and it was amazing to see the reviewers point out a passage of mine, as an example of Dickens's peculiar vein, and in the next sentence, comment on a paragraph of Dickens's, as a sample of Wilkie Collins's sensational style.'

Of his habits of writing, he mentions that he usually began work at about ten o'clock A.M., and wrote four or five hours per diem; more than that was apt to prove unprofitable, and required to be re-written. He is, we should judge, a pains-taking writer, having often to revise his proofs four or five times, before the work goes to press. He was educated as a lawyer as was Dickens, Charles Reade, Hepworth Dixon and other prominent English authors.

Mr. Collins expressed himself as much pleased with the New England scenery, and said it reminded him of some of the landscapes of northern Switzerland, in the region of the Jura Mountains, before one reaches the high Alps. On leaving our domain, he remarked that he thought it the most beautiful spot he had seen in America.

Mr. Collins thought our system of communism the most perfect democracy in existence, as it rated everyone exactly according to his or her merits, without any adventitious aids whatever. He thought there is a great need of social reform in England, and said that underneath the surface of society there is a great deal of seething and fermentation which is sure to break out at last, in some form or another. He had no doubt that a Community like ours would be tolerated in England, and mentioned the Agapemone[28] as a case in point. Altogether a more intelligent and pleasant visitor than Wilkie Collins, it has rarely been our fortune to entertain.[29]

Just as the members of the Wallingford Community had learned about Collins from his time among them, he too had garnered much from his visit. In the three hours that he spent with Charles Joslyn and the Perfectionists, he had gained such familiarity with the Community and its principles that he used Wallingford as the basis for Amelius Goldenheart's utopian home in his 1879 novel, *The Fallen Leaves*. In that book, Amelius's description of Tadmor reflects the Wallingford locale as Collins observed it:

A prettier place I never saw, and never expect to see again. A clear winding river, running into a little blue lake. A broad hill-side, all laid out in flower-gardens, and shaded by splendid trees. On the top of the hill, the buildings of the Community, some of brick and some of wood, so covered with creepers and so encircled with verandahs that I can't tell you to this day what style of architecture they were built in ...Visitors of all sorts are welcome at Tadmor. We have a large experience of them in the traveling season. They come with their own private suspicion of us lurking about the corners of their eyes. They see everything we have to show them, and eat and drink at our table, and join in our amusements, and get as pleasant and friendly with us as can be ...[30]

Collins's description of the beliefs held at his Tadmor, though recounted in Nordhoff's *The Communistic Societies of the United States*,[31] were first demonstrated to him at Wallingford. Five years later, after *The Fallen Leaves* had been published, he remembered the man who had shown him the characteristics of that socialistic lifestyle. Writing to Charles Joslyn, his guide at Wallingford, he revealed his obligation to the Community (Figure 11.2):

London 3rd April 1879

My dear Sir,

I have been away from London – and I hope you will excuse, on that account, my delay in thanking you for your kind letter.

The hospitable reception which I owed to your kindness at Wallingford is still fresh in my memory. Those traces of my appreciation of a very pleasant and interesting visit to your Community which you perceive in 'The Fallen Leaves,' have been purposely made vague traces. As your guest (though only the guest of a day!) I felt that it was part of my duty to you not to associate your Community too plainly with a work of fiction.

I live in the hope of visiting the United States again – though I cannot as yet see my way to a future day of departure from England. But, when I do find myself once more in New York, you may depend on it. I shall not fail to report myself. I am interested in the serious social experiments which have attained so large a measure of success among your Communistic Societies in America – and I should especially like to see [~~XXX~~] you all at Oneida.

Believe me,
Vy truly yours,
Wilkie Collins

To C. S. Joslyn Esq. [Secy] O. C.[32]

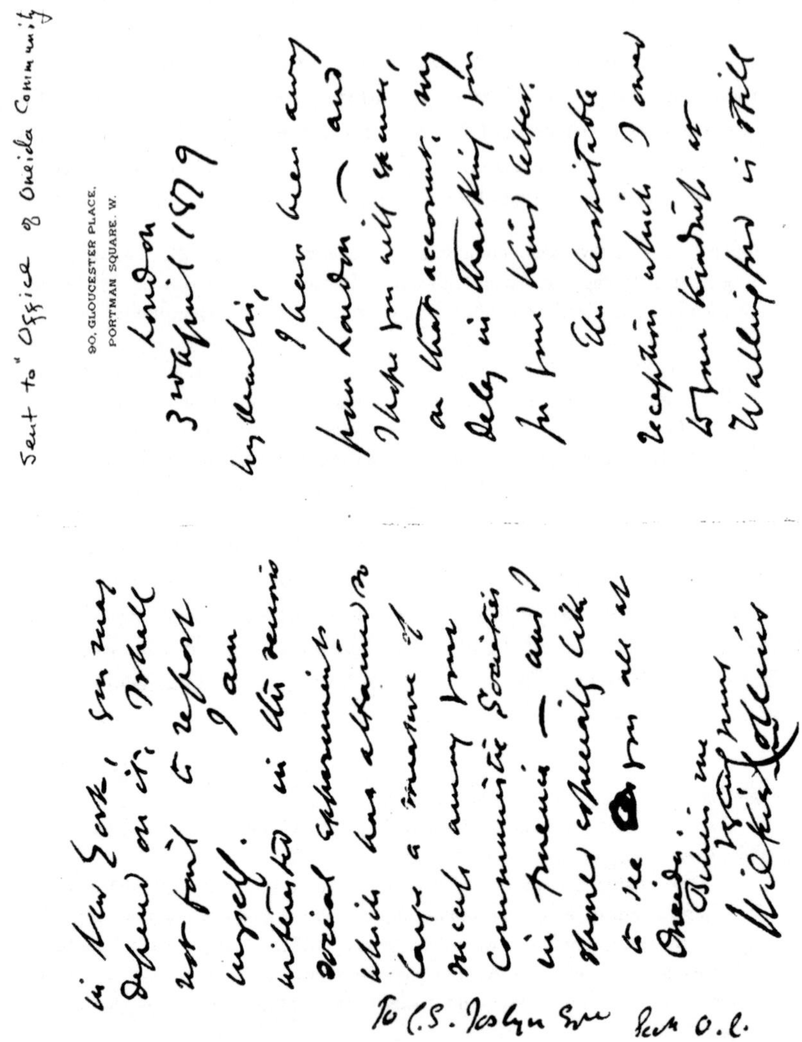
Sent to "Office of Oneida Community

90, GLOUCESTER PLACE.
PORTMAN SQUARE. W.

London
3rd April 1879

My dear Sir,
I have been away from London — and I hope you will excuse, on that account, my delay in thanking you for your kind letter.
The hospitable reception which I once owed to your kindness at Wallingford is still

in New York, you may depend on it. I shall not fail to report myself. I am interested in the serious social experiments which has attained so large a measure of success among your Communistic Societies in America — and I should especially like to see you all at Oneida.
Believe me
Vy truly yours
Wilkie Collins

To C.S. Joslyn Esq Secy O.C.

Figure 11.2: Collins revealed in this 1879 letter to Charles Joslyn that his visit to Wallingford had inspired *The Fallen Leaves* (Oneida Collection, Syracuse University, with permission).

Collins returned to Boston from New York City the next day. As in New York, the flurry of visits and preparations for departure sapped his time and energy. In spite of his efforts, he was unable to make a farewell call on Oliver Wendell Holmes,[33] and in a letter to Henry Longfellow, he regretted that 'numerous demands' left him 'no hope of being able to get to Cambridge and take your hand at parting'.[34] He wrote to William Seaver, asking him to send his 'kindest remembrances to all my friends in New York whom I have failed to see' and to look out for a possibility of employment for Ward, who had 'done his work admirably'.[35] He was also unable to visit George Childs again, but promised to 'return to my good American friends at the first opportunity that I can find'.[36]

On Saturday, 7 March, in a snowstorm, Collins bid farewell to America and set sail for England aboard the Cunard steamer *Parthia*, docking in Liverpool on 18 March. It was a safe and pleasant voyage, prompting him to recommended the line to William Seaver:

> N.B. Travel by Cunard – he takes soundings in a fog, and is not in such a damned hurry that he has no time to think of the lives of his passengers.[37]

CONCLUSION: WILKIE COLLINS AND THE AMERICAN PEOPLE

Was Wilkie Collins's American reading tour a success? Unfortunately, that question cannot be answered in an unequivocal affirmative. Whether it met his expectations will never fully be known. We have seen that his own descriptions of his public reception often contradicted the tone of newspaper reviews. His account, in a letter to Dion Boucicault, that he 'riveted' his Albany audience[1] contrasted with the newspaper review of that event that questioned his success as a speaker.[2] The reviewer in a New Bedford newspaper observed that Collins had 'no power of voice' and that it was lost to 'the ill-mannered crowd' while the same article reported that Collins was 'delighted with his audience'. In a letter written in 1874 by Mary Bradford, wife of painter William Bradford whom Collins had visited in New Bedford, she alludes to Collins's acceptance in America:

> Mr. Collins talked in highest terms of America and his reception there if some of our most respectable people did not see fit to admire him.[3]

He did not get to San Francisco to see his cousins, the Grays, and he did not even get as far as Utah, as he had written optimistically to Fred Lehmann. In spite of his allusions to the positive effect of the American climate on his health, he complained of the train journeys that sacrificed his ailing back to ceaseless jostling and his eardrums to the incessant clacking of the rails. He used the hardships of train travel as an excuse for the reduced number of speaking engagements he could consecutively manage.

Collins believed he had been cheated by the American Literary Bureau and had confronted unappreciative audiences and critical reviews. His problems with the American Literary Bureau had resulted in far fewer speaking engagements, and thus far less income, than he had anticipated. Bad press, both in reviewing his readings and in reporting exorbitant ticket prices and failed appearances, left a bad impression for both reader and audience. He made about £2,500,[4] nowhere near the £19,000 that Dickens brought back from America, or even the £9,500 earned by Thackeray. He had originally hoped that his success in America would enable him to repeat his readings once he returned to England but he never attempted to do so.[5] Nor did he ever return to the United States.

While his readings may not have been considered particularly successful, public fascination with Collins the novelist was pervasive. Newspapers continued mentioning him during the entire six months of his visit. Hardly a day went by that the newspapers failed to report his whereabouts or relay some pun or witticism about Wilkie Collins:

> Wilkie Collins will find himself known in America. In our large cities he will find the 'New Magdalen' at every turn.[6]
>
> Whatever may be said of Wilkie Collins's habits, we hope it will never be reported that he had been seen 'Moon-stone' – blind drunk.[7]
>
> Wilkie Collins wears specs, and will make another spec by his lectures.[8]
>
> Wilkie Collins was found by his Syracuse audience to be the counterfeit presentment of a local doctor. His phiz('ck') was exactly the same.[9]
>
> Wilkie Collins, at his recent reading in Troy, is said by a local paper to have been attired, with the exception of a dress-coat and white cravat, in the customary manner of men. They must have expected him to appear in tights, or at least, a costume of the sixteenth century.[10]
>
> Wilkie Collins wanted to see a band of real live Indians before leaving America, but had to be content with a peep at the New York murderers and Boston Aldermen.[11]
>
> It is announced that Wilkie Collins only comes to this country to get material for a story of American life. Let him visit the Modoc squaws and he will have abundant material for a 'Woman in Red.'[12]

Anecdotes circulated widely. In addition to the outrageously popular story of 'Wilkie Collins and the Inebriated Congressman', there were others:

> Wilkie Collins has a dish of cold roast beef continually on the sideboard of his room, so that he may replenish the inner man at stated intervals without having recourse to the hotel larder.[13]
>
> The scene at the Lotos Club, on Saturday night, where the reformer Bradlaugh shook hands for the first time with the novelist [Wilkie Collins], who he had long admired but could not meet on account of the tyranny of English social laws, was a most interesting and characteristic episode.[14]
>
> Wilkie Collins is so good-natured and so small that ladies ask him all sorts of naive questions.[15]
>
> Wilkie Collins was bothered by many beggars while in this country, one of whom offered to give him a powder to prolong his life to 150 years if he would pay $500 in consideration.[16]

It is clear that, in spite of his failure as a dramatic reader, the American public was captivated by Wilkie Collins, the celebrity. A month into his American tour, the *Rochester Union and Advertiser* observed,

> If there is any one thing more than another that Wilkie Collins will find to admire in this country, it will be these pen portraits of himself.[17]

In appearance, not only was he compared to Dickens,[18] Collins was also said to resemble 'the late Edward M. Stanton' (US Secretary of War),[19] 'the picture on the 50-cent scrip',[20] and both pictures of himself[21] and 'not quite what is suggested by his portraits'.[22] One reviewer summed up his looks as those of 'a hearty, whole-souled, thorough-going, vigorous, active gentleman'.[23]

Descriptions of his readings varied from 'he exhibited exceptionally fine powers',[24] 'his enunciation was clear and distinct',[25] and 'his voice [had] depth and volume'[26] to 'he was far from being faultless',[27] 'he was more colloquial than dramatic',[28] and finally to '[he was] unquestionably a failure'.[29]

But even after poor reviews began to circulate, his appearances drew crowds that came principally to see the great novelist rather than to attend his readings. He was swarmed by countless admirers and met some of the most influential men in the United States. He was extravagantly entertained and gloriously fêted. He learned about the American character and earned the admiration and respect of most everyone he met. He had the opportunity to witness the effect that his books had on a population that lionized him as the greatest living novelist.

He left the United States with the experience of travelling in a young, boisterous, and, sometimes, strange country. His encounters with the American people stimulated his mind and enriched his writing. While he was in the United States, he wrote his wrongful conviction thriller, *The Dead Alive*. His subsequent books continued to reflect his American experiences. *The Fallen Leaves* uses descriptions of a Utopian colony gleaned from his visit to the Wallingford Community. That experience also influenced *The Legacy of Cain*, where the villainess Helena becomes the leader of an American religious cult. A theme of *The Guilty River* deals with social equality, witnessed by him as he travelled in the United States during the period of Reconstruction. In *The Two Destinies* and *Blind Love*, America serves as a far-away place to transport characters to conveniently keep them from encountering each other. In 1885 he seriously considered writing an historical drama set in the US and starring American actress Mary Anderson, although he ultimately abandoned the project.[30]

Collins was present in America to witness his plays produced and special editions of his works published. In 1873, Harper & Brothers began issuing a seventeen-volume Illustrated Library Edition of his novels to commemorate his

American tour. The volumes included a portrait of the author by noted engraver Frederick Halpin and a facsimile inscription that read:

> I gratefully dedicate
> this collection of my
> Works, to
> The American People
> Wilkie Collins
> September 1873.

The same year, his Canadian publishers, Hunter, Rose, published five titles, including *American Readings* (that consisted of 'The Frozen Deep', and 'The Dream Woman',[31] read onstage), and William F. Gill published editions of his American readings as well.[32] T. B. Peterson of Philadelphia issued new – and unauthorized – editions of his works, a publishing occurrence that, unfortunately for Collins's wallet, was not unusual.

Perhaps Wilkie Collins best summarized his response to America in a letter to George Childs written from the *Parthia* as he sailed for home:

> *I leave you with a grateful heart – with recollections of American kindness and hospitality which will be, as long as I live, among the happiest recollections to which I can look back.*[33]

APPENDIX A: 'THE DREAM WOMAN'

An outline of Wilkie's reading of 'The Dream Woman' appeared with most newspaper reviews. This particular synopsis was the one most often reproduced in the papers.

> THE DREAM WOMAN, in four narratives. *Dramatis Personae* – Mr. Percy Fairbanks, an English gentleman; Mrs. Fairbanks, his wife; Alicia Warlock, the dream woman; Francis Raven, the groom; Riggobaud, a servant; M. Bernell, proprietor of a vineyard. The scene partly in England and partly in France.
>
> First narrative – conducted by Percy Fairbanks, an English gentleman who resides the greater part of the time in Farleigh Hall, England, but is obliged, in connection with his business, to make occasional visits to France. Mr. Fairbanks is traveling with his wife at the time the scene opens. One of his horses has fallen lame on the road, and what is to be done? They look around them, but see no signs of human habitation. There is a hill before; they ride to the top of this and see a town on the other side; it is the town of Underbridge, composed of one muddy street on which is situated the Eagle Inn. Leaving him in charge of the horses, Mrs. Fairbanks saunters down the yard, opens the door and peeps in.
>
> Mr. Fairbanks is on the point of calling the hostler, when he hears Mrs. Fairbanks's voice. Mrs. Fairbanks, it seems, has opened the last door at the end of the yard, and there she sees a strange sight – a dingy stable, and in one corner horses munching hay, and in another a man breathing convulsively. She calls to him, 'Wake up! Wake up!' but he only stirs restlessly in his sleep. While she watches him he mutters as if some vision was passing across his troubled brain.
>
> 'Fair hair, with yellow in it; gray eyes with a droop in the left eyelid; little hands pinned around the nails; a knife with a buckhorn handle – murder, murder!' Then he stops and grows restless.
>
> When he speaks again his tone is altered: 'Say you lovely being, I am so fond of you.' The words die on his lips; he speaks no more. Mrs. Fairbanks gets over her first terror excited by his words and calls her husband, tells him what she has heard and gives her opinion that there has been a murder committed, and requests him to go and get help. Just as he, yielding to her solicitations, is on the point of going he stumbles on a stranger at the stable door, a man who turns out to be the landlord of the inn.
>
> 'Good morning,' he says; 'I am a little hard o'hearing; say, did you call?'
>
> Mr. Fairbanks's wife interposes: 'Who is that man asleep on the straw? Did he fall in love with a murderess? Did she stab him or not?'

The old fellow waits till she's done and then says: 'His name is Francis Raven; forty-five years of age his last birthday; he is my brother.' The landlord then enters the stable and stirs the man up as if he were a wild beast. The man looks around him with a horrid glare of suspicion at first, and then becomes calm. They question him, ask him why he was asleep at that time of day. He replies that he was tired, and tired out.

'Tired out, eh? Hard work, I suppose?'

'No, sir.'

'Well, what then? Up all night? Nothing going on in this town, anybody ill?' 'Nobody ill, sir.' And they can get nothing more from him. Mrs. Fairbanks is not satisfied; he curiosity is aroused, and as he is to be their driver she places her husband behind and takes a seat besides the driver, and during the journey succeeds from the man his story. But now let Francis Raven tell his own story.

This is the story of Francis Raven – the second narrative: It is now ten years ago since I got the great warning of my life. Suppose yourself in a little cottage with me and my mother. We were talking about a great journey I was to take the next morning – the morning before my birthday – to a neighboring town, to get a place. My mother was dead set against this.

'You cannot walk there and back again by night,' she said, 'You will have to sleep away from home on your birthday.' I, however, held to my opinion, and set out the next morning, calling out as I left,

'I will get back in time for my birthday, never fear.' It was then the last day of February. Be pleased to remember that the first day of March was my birthday, and two o'clock in the morning the hour of my birth. I will tell you what happened on my journey. I reached the house and made application for the place, but found I had been anticipated and the place was already taken. Swallowing my disappointment, I made some inquiries at the inn and found that I could save some time by taking another route back. I started, but a storm came up and I lost my way and was forced to take refuge at an inn. Here I will say that I am a temperate man, and my supper that night consisted solely of a slice of bread and a small glass of wine. Nothing was said at the time which could in any way excite my mind; nothing to excite my mind to play tricks with my common sense. I got ready for bed; the wind was still; the storm had subsided. I read for some time by candle-light, and I finally fell asleep. The next thing that I was conscious of I was wide-awake, with a terrible shivering fit upon me, and a horrible sinking pain at my heart. My candle had burned low in the socket, and the last part of the wick had just fallen off, and there, between the foot of the bed and the closed door of the room was a woman, standing and looking fixedly at me, with a knife in her hand. I was struck speechless with terror. There the woman stood, with the knife in her hand, her eyes fixed upon me. She said nothing, but moved slowly towards the bed. I saw a fair, fine woman, with light gray eyes, with a droop in the left eyelid, and a knife with a buckhorn handle. She came round to the side of the bed without any change in the stony expression of her face; came nearer, nearer, with the knife raised to stab. As I saw it coming I jerked to the other side of the bed just as the knife descended. She drew the knife slowly out of the bed with her delicate white hands, with a flush under the fingernails. She went to the foot of the bed, stood there a moment, and then passed round to the other side and again struck at me. It was a large knife – such as men use to cut bread with – made of buckhorn, and looked as good as new. A second time she drew the knife out of the bed and hid it in the sleeve of her gown. At that moment the wick fell, there was a moment of darkness, and the woman with the knife was gone. When I came to myself my heart was beating violently, and I cried out,

'Wake up! Wake up! Murder! Murder!' I groped around the room and found the door; it was locked. Could she have come in at the window? That was locked too. Then the landlord came with a gun and a light.

'What is it?' said he. I told him there was a woman in the room with a knife in her hand. He looked at me a moment, and then said coldly, 'Well, she seems to have missed you.' I told him to look at the bed. He went and came back in a passion; there was no such thing as a cut of a knife on the bed. 'What do you mean,' he said, 'by a woman with a knife trying to stab you? Ho! Ho! It was a woman seen in a dream!'

What, a dream woman tried to stab me, not a living woman, not a living human being like myself! Horror got hold of me. I left the house and rushed out into the rain and home, and hardly knew how. I told my mother all that had happened. She asked me what time it was when I saw the woman. Allowing for the time it took me to get home, it must have been two o'clock in the morning – the morning of my birthday; and at the very hour of my birth.

My mother opened her desk and said, 'Tell me, my son, what she looked like.' I described her fully, as I have already described her to you – the light gray eyes with the droop in the left eyelid, and the knife with the buckhorn handle. My mother wrote it down carefully and put it away in her desk. This is the story of the warning. Now judge whether it is true or false when you know what happened on the next birthday. The night preceding my next birthday found me at the surgery in quest of medicine for my mother. While it was being prepared, a young woman entered the room and asked for laudanum. The doctor refused to sell her any, and I, fearing she intended to poison herself, against the advice of her doctor, followed her out and questioned her. She confessed the desperate strait to which she was reduced, and I – well, in a word, I fell madly in love with her, took her home with me, and, after a short time married her, against the advice of my mother, who thought she recognized in her 'The Dream Woman.' Her name was Alicia Warlock. Time passed on and she turned out to be a drunkard. Mother died, and my wife, in a state of intoxication, insisted on attending the funeral. I got angry with her, and in a fit of rage, I struck her. When I returned from the funeral, I found her awaiting me with a terribly calm and fixed expression upon her face. 'No man has ever struck me before,' she said, 'and my husband shall never have another opportunity.' She shut the door and I saw her go up the street. All that night I watched, but no one came. The next night, my slumbers were undisturbed, but on the seventh night I awoke again with that strange sinking at my heart. I looked and there was the Dream Woman again! No, but my own wife, with her arm raised in the attitude of the dream. I sprang for her, but she hid the knife in her sleeve, a knife with a buckhorn handle. It was all I could do to keep from dropping on the floor.

'You mean to kill me,' I said.

'Yes,' she replied, 'I did want to kill you with that knife.' I do not know what possessed me, but I acted like a coward and fell down, like a woman in a swoon. When I came to, the knife was nowhere to be seen; she had probably taken it with her. I opened the window; a policeman was going by. I asked him what time it was. Two o'clock in the morning; it was my birthday. The connection with the dream was complete. There was not a link wanting. That was my second warning. Since then, I have lived round from place to place, waiting for my next birthday, which I fear is to be the day of my death. My wife is looking for me. I don't believe in dreams. I only say that Alicia warlock is looking for me. I may be wrong, and may be right; which of you can tell? This is the end of the second narrative.

The third narrative is by Percy Fairbanks, who continues the story. He tells how he talked the matter over with his wife, and she desiring very much to have the servant in their employ till his next birthday, so that she might see what would happen. He yielded, and they took him with them to the south of France. Shortly before the time of his next birthday, he was so unfortunate as to have his leg broken by the kick of a horse, and he was laid up in consequence. The hostler was looking forward with much anxiety to the first of March, his birthday, and Mr. Fairbanks tried in vain to comfort him. The physician suggested that if the groom did not know that in that year, leap year, February had twenty-nine days he would have the climax of his fears at the wrong time. This turned out to be the case, and Mr. Fairbanks went to him on the morning of the 29th and rallied him on the groundlessness of his alarm, but the man only gave him a strange look and said that something was wrong.

At the time when the hostler was laid up, Mr. Fairbanks was driven, in consequence, to employ a French groom named Joseph Rygobaud. This man was left in charge of the hostler during the night preceding the first of March, and the testimony of this man before the judge forms the forth and concluding narrative. His testimony: I am thirty-two years old, a groom in the service of Mr. Fairbanks; remember the 27th of February of this year; I was on that day in the city of Metz, and there I met a charming lady. She was English, but could speak French as well as a native. The result of our interview was that she should meet me at this Maison Rouge at ten o'clock when the other servants had retired. She came, and I received her at supper in the room adjoining the apartment adjoining the apartment where the hostler was lying. As we were sitting down to supper, the sick man called out to me by name, and at the sound of his voice the lady became very much excited and inquired his name and what was the matter with him. On my telling her, she made me take her downstairs and show her which horse it was that had broken her brother's leg, and when I told her, she kissed him. Then she ran back upstairs, and I stayed to lock the stable. When I came up, I found the woman at the door of the sick man's room. I went in and found the man in a very excited condition, and he implored me not to leave him. He made such a noise that I went and got some handkerchiefs and gagged him. Then I heard my mistress call and I went away and left the woman there and the man thus bound. My mistress wanted to know how the man was getting along, and if anything had happened. I said,

'Nothing whatever, ma'am. If he is not disturbed, he will fall into a good sleep.'

I was on my way back to the room when I heard a sound like the cracking of a door on its hinges. I looked and found the west door open. I supposed it was the wind. I shut it and went in to look for the Englishwoman, but I could not find her. I then went to the hostler's room and listened. There was not a sound. I called, but there was no answer. A dim presentment of evil came over me. I opened the door and looked in. I noticed something dark creeping in a crevice of the floor near the door. I examined it closely. The dark moving object was a stream of blood. I rushed into the room and saw the Englishman stabbed in the head and heart. There was a knife lying near with a buckhorn handle.

'Have you anymore to tell me?' asked the Judge.

'No, nothing,' said the trembling man, 'except that I am innocent. Oh, Judge, don't send me to trial for murder.'

Upon this the Judge closed the examination and the prisoner was carried to his cell.

Percy Fairbanks then concludes:

Joseph Rygobaud was tried and found innocent. Of the woman Alicia Warlock, nothing more was heard, and it remains doubtful whether she died by drowning (as they traced her tracks near the river) or not. At any rate, she was never seen again. Thus the 'Dream Woman' passes from your view. Was she a ghost, a spirit, or a living woman? What was it? Remember that dreams are around you on every side, and the greatest of poets had written;

'We are such stuff
As dreams are made of; and our little life
I rounded with a sleep.'

APPENDIX B: PERFORMANCE SUMMARY

Date	**Place**	**Location**	**Cost**	**Reaction**	**Source**
7 October	Albany	Martin Opera House		all seats taken; 'very satisfactory'	*Evening Journal* (8 October)
8 October	Troy	Rand Hall		medium crowd; 'no actor or elocutionist'	*Daily Press* (10 October)
9 October	Utica	Opera House	$ 0.75–1.00	'paltry 400'; 'no elocutionist'	*Herald* (10 October)
11 October	Syracuse	Weiting Opera House	$ 0.50–0.75–1.00	small audience; 'a failure'	*Courier* (13 October)
13 October	Rochester	Corinthian Hall	$1.00	'Postponed due to illness'	*Union and Advertiser* (13 October)
17 October	Philadelphia	Horticultural Hall	$ 0.50–0.75–1.00	mixed reaction	*Press* / *Inquirer* (18 October)
30 October	Boston	Music Hall	$1.00	'packed hall'; 'thrilling'	*Transcript* (31 October)
11 November	New York	Association Hall	$1.50	mixed reaction	*Times* / *Herald* (12 November)
26 November	Baltimore	Masonic Temple	$1.00	'large audience'; 'fame ... carried him'	*Gazette* (27 November)
28 November	Washington DC	Lincoln Hall	$1.00		
11 December	Providence	Music Hall	$ 0.50–0.75	'pleasant but without power'	*Journal* (12 December)
18 December	New Bedford	Lyceum Hall		'large ill-mannered crowd'	*Republican Standard* (25 December)
22 December	Montreal	Queen's Hall	$ 0.75–1.00		

Date	Place	Location	Cost	Reaction	Source
26 December	Toronto	Music Hall	$ 0.50–0.75–1.00	'very full house'; 'lacks all elements'	*Leader* (27 December)
6 January	Buffalo	St. James Hall	$ 0.50	'standing room only'; voice clear'	*Express* (7 January)
8 January	Cleveland	Case Hall	$ 0.50–0.75–1.00	'very fair audience'; 'great interest'	*Leader* (9 January)
9 January	Sandusky	Opera House	$ 0.50–1.00	'very fair'; 'rapt attention'	*Register* (10 January)
12 January	Toledo	Wheeler Opera House	$ 0.50–1.00	'paucity' of audience	*Blade* (13 January)
13 January	Detroit	Opera House	$ 0.50–0.75	'small audience'; 'not even average'	*Free Press* (14 January)
16 January	Chicago	Music Hall	$ 0.50–1.00	'large appreciative'; 'more than fair'	*Inter-Ocean* (17 January)
30 January	Salem	Essex Institute	$ 0.50	'full hall' but 'least said the better'	*Post* (4 February)
31 January	Boston	Tremont Hall	$ 0.50	afternoon reading: 'good'	*Evening Traveller* (2 February)
5 February	Springfield	Opera House	$ 0.50–0.75	'well pleased'	*Daily Union* (6 February)
6 February	Worcester	Mechanics Hall	$ 0.50	'less than 500'; 'repulsive'	*Spy* (7 February)
27 February	Boston	Parker Hall	$ 0.50	'fine large aud'; 'rapt attn.'	*Evening Traveller* (28 February)

APPENDIX C: ITINERARY

Note: *L* indicates letter written to recipient.

September 1873

M	Tu	W	Th	F	Sa	Su
1	2	3	4	5	6	7
8	9	10	11 Signs new will	12 *L*:Tindell	13 Sails from Liverpool on *SS Algeria*	14 Sails from Queenstown Harbour at 4.00 p.m. for New York
15 At Sea	16	17	18 Financial Panic in U.S.	19	20	21
22	23	24	25 Arrives in New York; met by Fechter; dines at hotel	26 New York Westminster Hotel	27 New York Westminster Lotos Club Dinner at 9.00	28 New York Westminster With Reeve
29 New York Westminster At theatre 'Wrote to Mr Bigelow'	30 New York Westminster Dines with 'some men' *L:Jane Bigelow*					

October 1873

M	Tu	W	Th	F	Sa	Su
		1 New York John Bigelow calls at hotel; WC packing Century Club Dinner	2 Fechter's farm	3 Fechter's farm	4 Fechter's farm	5
6 Visits Bigelows at their country estate, 'The Squirrels'	7 Albany Delavan House First reading: Martin Hall	8 Albany Entertained by Gov. Dix *L: Boucicault* *L: Sherman* To Troy: Troy House Reading at Rand Hall	9 Troy Tour by Mr Littlefield; Receives Boorne book; Leaves at 2.00 p.m; Utica Reading at Opera House	10 Utica	11 Syracuse Reading: Wieting OperaHouse	12 Syracuse 'Sudden illness' reported in *Rochester Union* on 13 October
13 New York? Rochester reading 'post-poned'	14 New York?	15 New York? Reading scheduled at Williamsport, Pennsylvania	16 New York?	17 Philadelphia Reading at Horticul-tural Hall	18 Philadel-phia	19 Philadel-phia 'Delightful evening' with G. Childs in Philadel-phia
20 Philadelphia?	21 Returns to New York Westminster *L: G. Childs*; Medical consult	22 New York William Seav-er's Breakfast at the Union Club	23 New York	24 New York	25 New York *L: Unknown*	26
27 'Two days' moun-tain trip' apparently cancelled	28 Leaves for Boston; Tremont House Hotel	29 Boston Tremont Visit with James T. Fields; Attends opera	30 Boston Visits Fields Reading #1 *Dream Woman* at Music Hall *L: G. Towle*	31 Boston Cambridge for the day Dinner engagement in Boston *L: Schles-inger*		

November 1873

M	Tu	W	Th	F	Sa	Su
					1 New York? Reading? (says one was scheduled) *L: Unknown*	2 New York?
3 New York?	4 New York?	5 New York? Reading? (Says one was sched-uled)	6 New York?	7 New York?	8 New York?	9 New York Attends Mercantile Library Assn. dinner *L: C. Pascoe*
10 New York with F. Ward Attends opening of *The New Magdalen* at Broadway Theater	11 New York First NYC reading at Association Hall 8.00 *L: J. Bigelow* *L: W. Seaver*	12 New York	13 New York	14 New York *L: Hulburt* WC mentions invitation on the 15 November; Scheduled Worcester reading	15 New York Dines at Manhattan Club with Mr Hulburt	16 New York Ward goes back to Boston; Has dinner plans *L: Schleslinger*
17 New York?	18 New York?	19 New York?	20 New York?	21 New York Westminster *L: G. Bentley* *L: W. Tindell* Writes for seven hours	22 New York?	23 New York?
24 Leaves New York?	25	26 Baltimore At Car-rollton; Reading *L: J. Elder-kin* *L: Ward to Hunter Rose*	27 Baltimore City tour; Announced WC not coming to New Bedford	28 Washington Reception at Washington Club; Guest of Mr Philip Reading	29 Washington Visits National Theater with Maggie Mitchell	30

December 1873

M	Tu	W	Th	F	Sa	Su
1 Ward remains with WC	2 Returns from DC	3	4 New York with F. Ward Westminster *L: Ward to Rose*	5	6	7
8	9 New York Westminster *L: J. Redpath* *L: Unknown*	10 Boston Hotel St James	11 Providence Reading at Music Hall	12 Returns to Boston Announced to speak in Lockport	13 Boston Hotel St James *L: J. Thompson*	14
15 New York *Woman in White* opens on Broadway with Wybert Reeve as Fosco.	16 New York Redpath in Burlington *en route* to Montreal to make arrangements	17 Boston Hotel St James Dinner with Jere Abbott	18 New Bedford Reading; guest of William Bradford	19 Boston Leaves in the morning	20 Montreal	21 Montreal
22 Montreal Reading at Queen's Hall; Redpath's 'Card' in newspapers	23 Toronto Fifteen hours by train with Redpath	24 Toronto	25 Toronto Hunter Rose dinner *L: Schlesinger*	26 Toronto Reading at Music Hall, auspices of Mechanics Institute	27 Leaves for Niagara; Mr Smeaton assists at Custom House	28 Niagara
29 Buffalo Tifft House; Attends Savini's *Hamlet*	30 Buffalo Tifft House; Attends Shelby's 'Comique'	31 Buffalo Tifft House				

January 1874

M	Tu	W	Th	F	Sa	Su
			1 Buffalo Tifft House	2 Buffalo Tifft House Some leisure Torpedo visit *L: J. Harper* *L: H. Rose* *L: Lehmann*	3 Buffalo Tifft House Payson of Boston in Sandusky making arrangements	4 Buffalo Tifft House
5 Buffalo Tifft House *Dead Alive* published	6 Buffalo Tifft House Reading at St James Hall *L: F. Archer*	7	8 Cleveland Reading at Case Hall, managed by Redpath; fifti-eth birthday	9 Sandusky Lake House Reading at Opera House *L: G. Bentley*	10	11
12 Toledo Reading at Wheeler Opera House	13 Detroit Russell House; Reading at Opera House	14	15	16 Chicago Sherman House Reading at Music Hall Plans are uncertain *L: J. Harper*	17 Chicago Sherman House Will return to Boston *L: J. Bigelow* *L: L. Moulton* *L:Schlesinger*	18 Chicago Sherman House
19 Leaves Chi-cago Returns to Detroit	20 Detroit Russell House	21 Rochester Breaks trip	22 Boston Reported that western trip cancelled	23 Boston St James	24 Boston St James *L: J. Dwight*	25 Boston St James
26 Boston St James Dines with Harvard Musical Assn.	27 Boston St James *L: F. Archer* *L: W. Tindell*	28 Boston St James *L: Schlesinger*	29 Boston St James	30 Boston Salem Reading Essex InSt Train back to Boston	31 Boston Afternoon Reading #2 Tremont Temple Dinner with Schlesinger	

February 1874

M	Tu	W	Th	F	Sa	Su
						1 Boston St James *L: J. Harper*
2 Boston St James *L: W. Tindell*	3 Boston St James *L: C. Morse*	4 Boston St James	5 Springfield Haynes House Hotel Reading at Opera House Left at 1.30 By train	6 Worcester Reading at Mechanics Hall; delayed by rail accident	7	8 Boston Hotel Vendome
9 Boston Vendome Dinner with Charles Morse	10 Boston Vendome *L: J. Redpath* re. *Williams/Parry issue*	11	12	13	14	15
16 Boston Vendome Banquet at St James's Hotel given by Gill	17 Boston Vendome *L: Schlesinger*	18 Boston Vendome Dinner with Schlesinger	19 Boston?	20 Boston?	21 Boston Vendome Dined with Longfellow at Craigie House	22 Boston Vendome *L: J. Trowbridge*
23 Boston?	24 Boston?	25 Boston?	26 Boston?	27 Boston Farewell #3 reading at Parker Hall, *Frozen Deep* *L: C. Ward*	28 Boston Saturday Club with Gill	

March 1874

M	Tu	W	Th	F	Sa	Su
						1 New York Westminster Hotel
2 New York Westminster Says he just returned from Boston *L: J. Bigelow* *L: C. Ward* *L: J. Harper*	3 New York Westminster Calls in a.m. to Joseph Harper; Bigelows' between 2.00 and 3.00; Dines with Fechter and *L: W. Tindell*	4 New York Westminster Visits Wall- ingford; Arrives by noon train	5 Leaves New York for Boston	6 Boston *L: Longfellow* 'Numerous demands on my time' Twice tries to see Holmes; busy with preparations	7 Sails from Boston on the *S.S.* *Parthia* at 11.00 a.m. Friends see him off ... in a snowstorm *L: O. Holmes* *L: Schlesinger* *L: W. Seaver*	8 At Sea
9	10	11	12	13	14	15
16 At Sea *L: G. Childs* *L: C. Field*	17	18 Arrives at Liverpool	19	20	21	22
23	24	25	26	27	28	29
30	31					

APPENDIX D: CONTACTS

Attendees at Lotos Club Dinner in New York, 29 September 1873

[*] indicates speechmaker:

Andrews, William Symes: (1847–1929) pioneer electrical engineer for General Electric.

Appleton, William Henry: (1814–99) president of the publishers Appleton & Company and proponent of international copyright agreements.

***Botta, Vincenzo**: (b. 1818) professor of Philosophy from the University of Turin, he settled in New York in 1853 and filled the chair of Italian language and literature of the University of the City of New York.

Bouton, John R.

***Bradlaugh, Charles**: (1833–91) British politician, free thinker and radical lecturer who made financially unsuccessful tours of the US in 1874 and 1875.

Brelsford, Charles S.: president of the American Literary Bureau; he was Collins's first manager for his American reading tour.

***Brougham, John**: (1810–80) Irish actor and playwright, spending almost fifty years as a theatre professional in England and the US. He was a founder and early president of the Lotos Club.

Campanini, Signor: Italian operatic tenor who toured the US during 1873.

Carleton, Will: (b. 1845) Lyceum lecturer, traveller and author of popular ballads of domestic life, one of which, *Farm Ballads*, was published in New York in 1873.

Chamberlain, Ivory: American journalist and editorialist for the *New York World* and the *New York Herald*.

Chapin, John R.: (1823–1904) designer, painter, illustrator, and engraver, he was noted for his Civil War illustrations and his western scenes.

***Chapin, Dr. Edwin Hubbell**: (1814–80), pastor of the Church of Devine Paternity in New York.

Cleveland, Frank F.: (1853–93), president of Union Ironworks.

Conant, Samuel Stilman: (b. 1831), managing editor of *Harper's Weekly* from 1869 until January 1885 when he mysteriously disappeared.

Croly, David Goodman: (1829–89) Irish-born journalist and radical social thinker who founded the *Daily Graphic*, the nation's first illustrated daily, in 1873.

Devlin, John E.: New York statesman.

Forest, M. de la: Consul General of France.

Fulton, Chandos: author; wrote *A Brown Stone Front* in 1873.

Gedney, Frederick G.: Civil Justice and author of *Shenandoah*.

Gilbert, John: (1810–89) Boston actor who joined the company of Wallack's theatre in 1862 and remained connected with that company for the rest of his life.

Harte, Francis Bret: (1836–1902) American author. He founded the *Overland Monthly* in 1868 in which 'The Luck of Roaring Camp' was published, which began his career as a writer. In 1871 he moved from California to Boston where he became intimate with Emerson, Longfellow and Lowell. At that time, he took to lecturing as a means of earning income, but was not successful in that venture.

Hay, John Milton: (1838–1905) diplomat and author. He served as a colonel in the Civil War, after which he became a minor diplomat, securing posts in Paris, Vienna and Madrid. In 1870 he was hired by Whitelaw Reid as editorial writer for the *New York Tribune,* where he remained until 1875. He went on to become Assistant Secretary of State and later was appointed US Ambassador to Great Britain in 1897.

Kennett, Thomas A.: (1843–1911) physician.

Lumley, Arthur.: American landscape artist and book illustrator.

*__McDowell, Irvin__: (1818–85) major general who succeeded General George Meade as Commander of the Division of the South in 1872.

Nanetti, Signor: Italian operatic basso who toured the US during 1873.

Olcott, Henry Steel: (1832–1907) co-founder and president of the Theosophical Society, and an advocate of Buddhism. In the Civil War, he served as an investigator of fraudulent military suppliers, earning the rank of Colonel. He wrote extensively about spirit manifestations in early 1870s.

Palmer, Harry: manager of Union Square Theater of New York.

Pardee, Dr Charles Inslee: New York physician and Dean of University Medical College from 1877 to 1897.

Perry, Edward Aylesworth: (1833–89) brigadier general during the Civil War; he later became Governor of Florida in 1885.

***Phelps, B. K.**: District Attorney of New York.

Phillips, Frederick G.

Reeve, Wybert: (1831–1906) actor and friend of Collins; he played both Hartright and Fosco in *The Woman in White* and joined Collins on his reading tour of America.

Regamey, Felix: (1844–1907) French painter, draughtsman, writer, and something of an ethnographer. He espoused the European vogue of 'Japonisme'.

***Reid, Whitelaw**: (1837–1912) journalist, politician and diplomat. In 1868, he joined the staff of the *New York Tribune* under Horace Greeley. He was Greeley's campaign manager when he ran against President Ulysses Grant and took over the *Tribune* after Greeley's death. He was offered several diplomatic posts under President Garfield but he refused them, remaining in New York where he continued to gain fame and fortune. He reluctantly accepted the position of Minister to France in 1889.

Richards, Thomas Addison: (b. 1820) London-born artist and illustrator. In 1867 he became a professor of art at the University of the City of New York.

***Roosevelt, Robert Barnwell**: (b. 1829) lawyer and congressman, elected as a Democrat from New York in 1870.

Salvini, Alessandro: brother of Tommaso Salvini.

***Salvini, Tommaso**: (b. 1830) Italian tragedian. In 1873–4 he made a tour in the US in which he gave 128 Shakespearian performances.

***Saxe, John Godfrey**: (1816–87) lawyer and poet. In 1872 he became the editor of the *Albany Evening Journal*, but he achieved his greatest reputation with his poetry.

Schwab, Frederick A.: entertainment manager.

Scribner, John Blair: (d. 1879) head of the publishing firm of Charles Scribner's Sons.

Seaver, Col. William A.: (d. 1883) well-known New York *raconteur*; writer of the 'Editor's Drawer' of *Harper's Magazine*. He became a close friend to Collins.

Sexton, Samuel: prominent physician and surgeon; head of the New York Ear Dispensary and writer for *Harper's*.

***Stedman, Edmund Clarence**: (1833–1908) poet, critic and stockbroker. He became a New York journalist in the late 1850s, and published a book of poetry in 1860. He opened his own brokerage firm in 1864 but continued to write poetry and criticism and to mentor young poets.

Stillson, Jerome B.: (1841–80) New York journalist. He was managing editor of the *New York World* and worked on the *New York Herald.*

Stoddard, Richard Henry: (1825–1903) poet, critic and editor. He published a book of poems in 1852 and considered himself primarily a poet. He was appointed an inspector at the New York Custom House in 1853 where he remained until 1870, while at the same time working as a literary reviewer for the *New York World.* From 1870 to 1873 he acted as confidential secretary to General McClellan at the New York Department of Docks.

Sweet, Clinton W.: publisher and founder of *Real Estate Record,* a successful trade paper.

Taylor, J. B.: physician specializing in contagious diseases; Inspector of Vaccination.

Wieniawski, Henri: concert violinist.

Youmans, Edward Livingston: (1821–87) editor and doctor of medicine, though he did not practise. Instead he embarked on careers as a lecturer on the lyceum circuit and as a writer on scientific topics. He founded the *Popular Science Monthly* magazine in 1873.

Attendees at the Century Club Dinner in New York, 1 October 1873

Brundy, J. M.

Chamberlain, Ivory: *see above.*

Clantorsh, Hooper

Church, William Conant: (1836–1917) American editor; he became publisher of the *New York Sun* in 1860, later worked for the *New York Times,* and founded the *Galaxy* magazine in 1866.

Collins, Charles: (1813–75) educator; president of Emory and Henry College, Dickinson College and in 1860, State Female College of Tennessee.

Conant, Samuel Stillman: host of the affair; *see above.*

Deny, C. P.

Drisler, Henry: (1818–97) professor of Latin and Greek at Columbia University; Dean of the Faculty of Arts.

Fellarbury, F.

Godkin, Edwin Lawrence: (1831–1902) American publicist; wrote for the *London News* and the *New York Times* until 1865 when he founded the New

York *Nation.* He later became editor in chief of the *New York Evening Post,* in 1883.

Goodwin, Parke: (b. 1816) editor of the *New York Evening Post* and *Putnam's Monthly.*

Harper, John: (d. 1875) founder and financial officer of Harper & Brothers.

Harte, Bret: *see above.*

Hay, John: *see above.*

Holt, Henry: (1840–1926) author of novels and autobiographical works, and publisher of textbooks.

Lewis, Charlton Thomas: (d. 1904) lawyer, educator, lecturer in insurance matters; he wrote *Harper's Latin Dictionary* and *Harper's Book of Facts.*

Marbury, Francis F.: (d. 1895) lawyer and leading authority on maritime law.

Nast, Thomas: (1840–1902) caricaturist and political cartoonist; he drew for *Harper's Weekly* from 1859 to 1860 and from 1862 to 1886; for *New York Illustrated News* from 1860 to 1862.

Parton, James: (1822–1891) English-born author; he wrote biographies of Horace Greeley and Andrew Jackson.

Pectman, Edmund C.

Prime, Rev. Dr. Samuel Irenaus: (1812–85) Presbyterian minister and editor of the *New York Observer.*

Reid, Whitelaw: *see above.*

Seaver, Col. William A.: *see above.*

Seymour, Edward Woodruff: (1832–92) statesman, congressman from Connecticut and Connecticut Supreme Court Justice.

Smith, Augustine: (1821–97) vice president of Nassau Bank; partner of Campbell and Smith paper manufacturers.

Stedman, Edmund Clarence: (1833–1908) journalist and poet; contributed to *Vanity Fair* and *Harper's Magazine.* He was the news correspondent for *New York World.*

Stoe, Richard M.

Stoddard, Richard Henry: *see above.*

Thompson, Launt: (1833–94) Irish sculptor and portrait painter; vice president of the National Academy of Design from 1872 to 1873.

Attendees at the Union Club Breakfast in New York, 22 October 1873

Brougham, John: *see above.*

Bryant, William Cullen: (1794–1878) poet and journalist; owner and editor in chief of the *New York Evening Post.*

Cox, Samuel Sullivan: (1824–89) congressman from New York for thirty-five years.

Foster, John Gray: (1823–74) brigadier general and Civil War hero; he later served as superintending engineer for river and harbour improvements at Boston and Portsmouth.

Godwin, Parke: *see above.*

Harper, Joseph W.: (d. 1896) eldest of the Harper brothers.

Harper, Fletcher: (1806–77) publisher; head of Harper & Brothers after death of James Harper.

Hay, John: *see above.*

Hurlburt, E. P.

Holmes, Oliver Wendell: (1809–94) physician, professor of anatomy, writer and poet; co-founder of *Atlantic Monthly.*

Hutchings, Mr: judge of Surrogate Court.

Ingersoll, Charles Roberts: (b. 1821) elected Governor of Connecticut in 1873.

Loederer, Baron: Minister of Austria to Washington.

Polo de Barnabe, Admiral: Minister of Spain to Washington.

Attendees at the St. James Banquet in Boston, February 16, 1874

Clemens, Samuel Langhorne [Mark Twain]: (1835–1910) American humorist, satirist, writer and lecturer.

Gill, William F.: Boston publisher.

Higginson, Thomas Wentworth: (1823–1911) theologian, reformer, soldier and author; co-editor of *Woman's Journal* from 1870 to 1884.

Holmes, Oliver Wendell: *see above.*

Longfellow, Henry Wadsworth: (1807–82) American poet, educator, and linguist.

Quincy, Josiah: (1845–9) Mayor of Boston.

Whipple, Edwin Percy: (1819–86) essayist and critic, literary editor of *Boston Globe.*

Whittier, John Greenleaf: (1807–92) poet, abolitionist and journalist; co-founder of *Atlantic Monthly.*

Wilson, Henry: (1812–75) US Senator from Massachusetts and Vice-President of the United States under Grant.

APPENDIX E: PRESS PORTRAITS

A month into Wilkie's American tour, the *Rochester Union and Advertiser* observed,

> If there is any one thing more than another that Wilkie Collins will find to admire in this country, it will be these pen portraits of himself.[1]

This prescient statement is confirmed by a comparison of press reviews along the course of his tour:

Wilkie Collins was described as:

> a short, thick-necked man of five feet four[2]
> small in stature[3]
> medium in height[4]
> rather below the medium size[5]
> a rather tall man[6]
> one of the most diminutive specimens[7]
> an undersized gentleman[8]
> small and podgy[9]
> a fine bred man of medium size[10]
> rather under the usual height[11]
> above what is called the medium height[12]
> what he lacks in height he makes up in breadth;[13]

his beard was:

> bushy and white[14]
> full grey[15]
> slightly tinged with grey[16]
> full black, flecked with grey;[17]

he resembled:

> the late Edward M. Stanton [US Secretary of War][18]
> Dickens[19]
> Dr. Pease [of Syracuse][20]
> a not very distinguished person[21]
> the picture on the 50-cent scrip[22]

pictures of him[23]
not quite what is suggested by his portraits[24]
a hearty, whole-souled, thorough-going, vigorous, active gentleman;[25]

regarding his manner:

his walk was of a tip-toe fashion ... mincing[26]
[he had] a vigorous look and manner of walking[27]
he tripped across the stage[28]
he stepped into view with [a] swinging step[29]
[he was] slightly stooping in the shoulders[30]
he stepped ...with a firm, quick step[31]
[he] was as natural as ... a child;[32]

and as a reader:

he exhibited exceptionally fine powers[33]
he was far from being faultless[34]
he was more than fair[35]
[he had] a monotonous cockney accent[36]
he read in a very clear and distinct manner[37]
[he] emphasized ... unimportant words[38]
his enunciation was clear and distinct[39]
he was more colloquial than dramatic[40]
his voice [had] depth and volume[41]
his style of reading was very quiet[42]
he was distinctly audible[43]
his voice was too low for our great halls[44]
[he] succeeded better than was expected[45]
[he was] unquestionably a failure.[46]

NOTES

Preface

1. Wilkie Collins, quoted in L. B. Walford, *Memories of Victorian London* (London: Arnold, 1912), p. 209.
2. G. Dolby, *Dickens As I Knew Him* (London: T. Fisher Unwin, 1885).
3. E. Crowe, *With Thackeray in America* (London: Cassell and Company, 1893).
4. C. K. Hyder, 'Wilkie Collins in America', in *Studies in English in Honour of Raphael Dorman O'Leary and Seldon Lincoln Whitcomb* (Lawrence: University of Kansas, 1940), pp. 50–8.
5. K. Robinson, *Wilkie Collins: A Biography* (London: Bodley Head, 1951).
6. N. P. Davis, *The Life of Wilkie Collins* (Urbana: University of Illinois Press, 1956).
7. C. Peters, *The King of Inventors: A Life of Wilkie Collins* (Princeton, NJ: Princeton University Press, 1991).
8. W. Clarke, *The Secret Life of Wilkie Collins* (Stroud, Gloucester: Sutton, 2004).
9. M. K. Bachman and D. R. Cox (eds), *Reality's Dark Light: The Sensational Wilkie Collins* (Knoxville: University of Tennessee Press, 2003).
10. L. Pykett, *Wilkie Collins* (Oxford: Oxford University Press, 2005).
11. L. Nayder, *Wilkie Collins* (New York: Twayne, 1997).
12. J. B. Taylor (ed.), *The Cambridge Companion to Wilkie Collins* (New York: Cambridge University Press, 2006).
13. *The Public Face of Wilkie Collins*, ed. W. Baker, A. Gasson, G. Law and P. Lewis (eds), 4 vols (London: Pickering & Chatto, 2005).
14. *The Letters of Wilkie Collins*, ed. W. Baker and W. M. Clarke, 2 vols (Houndmills: Macmillan, 1999).

Introduction

1. *Charles Dickens: The Public Readings*, ed. P. Collins (Oxford: Clarendon Press, 1975), p. 52.
2. Ibid., p. 59.
3. J. L. Fisher (ed.), *Lives of Victorian Literary Figures V, Vol. 3: William Thackeray* (London: Pickering & Chatto, 2007), pp. 122–3.
4. G. W. Curtis, *Literary and Social Essays* (New York: Harper & Brothers, 1894), p. 130.
5. C. E. Norton, 'Charles Dickens', *North American Review*, 106 (April 1868), pp. 671–2; p. 671.

6. Dolby, *Dickens as I Knew Him*, p. 332.
7. A. G. Ray, *The Lyceum and Public Culture* (East Lansing: Michigan State University Press, 2005), p. 5.
8. *Edwardsville (Illinois) Intelligencer*, 10 July 1873.
9. Golconda was a fortress city west of Hyderabad, India, which, because of its diamond trade, became synonymous with vast wealth.
10. *Toronto Daily Globe*, 25 December 1873.

1 First Considerations of an American Tour

1. *The Letters of Charles Dickens and Wilkie Collins*, ed. L. Hutton (New York: Harper, 1892), pp. 153–4.
2. Ibid., p. 157.
3. Ibid., p. 160.
4. *Appleton's Journal* (3 September 1870).
5. Augustus Frederick Lehmann (1826–91) was the son of a Hamburg merchant who moved to Edinburgh and later London, becoming a part of literary circles in both. He and his wife, Nina, were Collins's lifelong friends.
6. John Bigelow (1817–1911) was an American editor, author and diplomat. From 1848 to 1861 he edited the *New York Evening Post* where he shared his anti-slavery and free trade views. He served as US minister to France in from 1865 to 1866. He found in Paris the original manuscript of Benjamin Franklin's *Autobiography*, which he edited and published in 1868. His other works include a life of Franklin which he published in 1874.
7. James Thomas Fields (1817–81) was an American author and publisher. He was the junior partner of Ticknor and Fields, a noted Boston publishing house in the mid-nineteenth century. He edited (1861–70) the *Atlantic Monthly* with notable success. His books, largely reminiscences of literary friendships, include *Yesterdays with Authors* (1872), *Hawthorne* (1876), and *In and Out of Doors with Charles Dickens* (1876).
8. George Makepeace Towle (1841–93) was an author and diplomat. He was US consul at Nantes, France, from 1866 to 1868, then transferred to the consulate at Bradford, England. He served as President of the Papyrus Club of Boston in 1880. He was managing editor of the *Boston Commercial Bulletin* from 1870 to 1871 and then was foreign editor of the *Boston Post.*
9. *Letters of Wilkie Collins*, vol. 1, p. 209.
10. Ibid., vol. 2, p. 351.
11. *New York Times*, 1 December 1872.
12. *New York Times*, 16 March and 23 May 1873.
13. *Harper's Weekly*, 8 March 1873, p. 1.
14. Wybert Reeve (1831–1906), Collins's actor friend who originally played Walter Hartright in *The Woman in White* in 1871, taking over the role of Fosco in 1872. He spent much of his life touring the US and Australia.
15. W. Reeve, 'Recollections of Wilkie Collins', *Chambers's Journal*, 9 (December 1905–November 1906), pp. 458–61; p. 460.
16. This might be Mrs Anne Edge Cunliffe, wife of the wealthy merchant banker Roger Cunliffe and mother of Walter Cunliffe, future governor of the Bank of England. See *Public Face of Wilkie Collins*, vol. 2, p. 385.
17. Ibid.

18. George Bentley (1828–95) was a member of the Bentley Publishing dynasty who first called Collins 'The King of Inventors'.
19. *Public Face of Wilkie Collins*, vol. 2, p. 386.
20. Ibid., vol. 2, p. 408.
21. Ibid., vol. 2, p. 408.
22. *New York World*, 23 September 1973, p. 4.
23. *New York Times*, 17 May 1874, p. 4.
24. *Baltimorean*, 31 May 1874, p. 4.
25. Wilkie Collins, letter to Joseph J. Casey, 12 July 1873. Simon Gratz Collection (ex. American Poets), Historical Society of Pennsylvania.
26. J. H. Harper, *House of Harper: A Century of Publishing in Franklin Square* (New York: Harper, 1912), p. 347.
27. *Public Face of Wilkie Collins*, vol. 2, p. 404.
28. Peters, *King of Inventors*, p. 346.
29. P. Fitzgerald, *Memoirs of an Author*, 2 vols (London: R. Bentley and Sons, 1894), vol. 1, p. 88.
30. F. Archer, *An Actor's Notebooks* (London: Paul, 1912), p. 152.
31. *Atlanta Constitution*, 23 July 1873.
32. *Atlanta Constitution*, 6 August 1873.
33. *Lafayette (Louisiana) Advertiser*, 9 August 1873 and *Fort Wayne (Indiana) Gazette*, 11 August 1873.
34. *Frank Leslie's Illustrated Newspaper*, 13 September 1873, p. 7.
35. *Boston Daily Globe*, 11 August 1873.

2 Underway to America

1. 'Morganatic', meaning a marriage with a person of lower rank, is the word that Collins used with Fred Lehmann and Sebastian Schlesinger to describe his relationship with Martha Rudd.
2. *Public Face of Wilkie Collins*, vol. 2, p. 306.
3. *Letters of Wilkie Collins*, vol. 2, p. 366.
4. *Detroit Evening News*, 23 January 1874, p. 4.
5. *Public Ledger Almanac* (Philadelphia, PA: Childs, 1874), p. 38.
6. *Letters of Wilkie Collins*, vol. 2, p. 67.
7. H. Zinn, *A People's History of the United States* (New York: HarperCollins, 2003), p. 242.
8. *Frank Leslie's Illustrated Newspaper Supplement*, 4 October 1873, p. 67.
9. *New York Times*, 26 September 1873, p. 8.
10. Charles Albert Fechter (1824–79) was an Anglo-French actor who began his career with the study of sculpture, but had a natural inclination for the stage. He astonished London playgoers with his interpretations of *Hamlet* and *Othello*. He toured the United States in 1869 as Hamlet. He returned to the United States in 1872, and purchased a farm in Pennsylvania. Wherever he appeared, he commanded large audiences, but his American career was not a success. He became ill and corpulent, and died on his farm.
11. W. Collins, 'Wilkie Collins's Recollections of Charles Fechter', in K. Field, *Charles Albert Fechter* (New York: Blom [1882] 1969), p. 172.
12. *New York World*, 26 September 1873, p. 5.
13. *New York Herald*, 26 September 1873, p. 3.

14. Collins, 'Recollections of Charles Fechter,' p. 172.
15. Ancestry.com, *Boston Passenger Lists, 1820–1891* (database on-line). Provo, UT. Microfilm roll number M277–87.
16. Reeve, 'Recollections of Wilkie Collins,' p. 460.
17. *New York Herald*, 27 September 1873, p. 10.

3 An Auspicious Welcome

1. J. Elderkin, *A Brief History of the Lotos Club* (New York: The Club, 1895), pp. 8–9.
2. J. Garraty and M. C. Carnes (eds), *American National Biography*, 24 vols (New York: Oxford University Press, 1999), vol. 3, p. 638.
3. Invitation to Lotos Club Dinner, 27 September 1873, Wilkie Collins, New York Public Library Special Collections.
4. A list of those in attendance, as determined from numerous newspaper reports, appears in Appendix D.
5. Elderkin, *Brief History of the Lotos Club*, p. 27.
6. *New York Sunday Mercury*, 28 September 1873.
7. *New York Herald*, 28 September 1873.
8. Reeve, 'Recollections of Wilkie Collins,' p. 460.
9. T. Reed (ed.), *Modern Eloquence: After-Dinner Speeches A-D* (Philadelphia, PA: John Morris, 1900), p. 261.
10. *New York World*, 28 September 1873.
11. Elderkin Speeches at the Lotos Club, 1901, in Reed, *Modern Eloquence*, pp. 261–2.
12. *New York Sunday Mercury*, 28 September 1873.
13. *New York Journal*, 28 September 1873.
14. *New York Tribune*, 29 September 1873.
15. Ibid.
16. *Kingston (Ontario) Whig*, 7 October 1873.
17. *Commercial Advertiser*, 29 September 1873.
18. Reeve, 'Recollections of Wilkie Collins,' p. 460.
19. *Public Face of Wilkie Collins*, vol. 2, p. 419.
20. *Detroit Free Press* Supplement, 18 January, 1874, vol. 1, quoted from *The Golden Age*.
21. Harper, *House of Harper*, p. 343.
22. Walford, *Memories of Victorian London*, pp. 208–9.
23. K. Baedaker, *The United States, with an Excursion into Mexico: Handbook for Travellers*, 1st edn (Leipsic: Baedeker, 1893), p. 30
24. Reeve, 'Recollections of Wilkie Collins,' p. 460.
25. Baedaker, *The United States*, pp. 30–1.
26. *Men and Women: A Weekly Biographical and Social Journal*, 5 February 1887, p. 282.
27. Journal of John Bigelow, 5 October, 1873. John Bigelow Papers, Manuscripts and Archives Division, New York Public Library, Astor, Lenox and Tilden Foundations.
28. *New York World*, 2 October 1873, p. 5.
29. Elderkin, *Brief History of the Lotos Club*, p. 8.
30. The guest list is included in Appendix D.
31. John Parton, letter to Ellen, 10 January 1874. Family papers, bMS Am 1248.4, Houghton Library, Harvard College Library.

32. *The Letters of William Cullen Bryant*, ed. W. C. Bryant II and T. Voss (New York: Fordham University Press, 1992), p. 137.
33. *New York World*, 2 October 1873, p. 5.
34. Menu, Collins, W. Collection, Pierpont Morgan Library.
35. *New York World*, 2 October 1973, p. 5.
36. The Pierpont Morgan Library, New York. MA Unassigned.
37. *New York World*, 2 October 1873, p. 5.
38. *New York Daily Graphic*, 3 October 1873, p. 658.
39. W. R. Mercer, 'Notes on the Life of Charles Albert Fechter', in *A Collection of Papers Read Before the Bucks County Historical Society* (Bucks County, PA: The Bucks County Historical Society), p. 504.
40. *Public Face of Wilkie Collins*, vol. 2, p. 420.
41. Collins, 'Recollections of Charles Fechter', p. 172.

4 The Tour Begins: Upstate New York

1. *Public Face of Wilkie Collins*, vol. 2, pp. 62–3. It can be surmised from their correspondence that Wilkie was attracted to the beautiful and vivacious Jane Bigelow. The first letter he sent her, after their meeting at John Foster's home, consisted of his transcription of a rather flirtatious excerpt from *The Woman in White*:

    Think of her as you thought of the first woman who quickened the pulses within you that the rest of her sex had no art to stir. Let the kind, candid blue eyes meet yours, as they met mine, with the one matchless look, which we both remember so well. Let her voice speak the music that you once loved best, attuned as sweetly to your ear as to mine. Let her footstep, as she comes and goes, in these pages, be like that other footstep to whose airy fall your own heart once beat time. Take her as the visionary nursling of your own fancy; and she will grow upon you, all the more clearly, as the living woman dwells in mine. (from chapter 8, describing Walter Hartright's first meeting with Laura Fairlie)

2. 'Authors at Home', *News of the Highlands*, 17 August 1900.
3. Henry Huntington (1850–1927) was a railroad magnate and business leader whose home and collections formed the basis for the Huntington Library.
4. J. Bigelow, *Retrospections of an Active Life*, 5 vols (Garden City, NY: Doubleday, 1913), vol. 5, p. 129.
5. Journal of John Bigelow. (Note: the diary entry was dated Tuesday, 8 October but the actual date would have been Tuesday, 7 October.)
6. Ibid.
7. *Albany Argus*, 8 October 1873, p. 4.
8. *Albany Evening Journal*, 8 October 1873, p. 4.
9. Ibid., p. 3.
10. Ibid., p. 3.
11. *Albany Argus*, 8 October 1873, p. 4.
12. Dionysius Lardner Boucicault (1820–90) was an Irish born dramatist, actor and man of the theatre whose career highlight was his play *The Shaughraun*, which opened in late 1874 in New York to extraordinary acclaim.
13. *Public Face of Wilkie Collins*, vol. 2, p. 420.

14. *Boston Daily Globe*, 9 October 1873, p. 1.
15. *Albany Argus*, 8 October 1873, p. 4.
16. Ibid., p. 4.
17. *Troy Daily Press*, 9 October 1873, p. 3.
18. *Troy Daily Press*, 10 October 1873, p. 1.
19. Ibid., p. 3.
20. *Troy Daily Times*, 9 October 1873, p. 3.
21. *Public Face of Wilkie Collins*, vol. 2, p. 430. The pamphlet was *The Trial, Confessions, and Conviction of Jesse and Stephen Boorn for the Murder of Russell Colvin, and the Return of the Man Supposed to Have Been Murdered*, by Leonard Sergeant.
22. *Troy Daily Times*, 16 May 1864. Captain J. F. Thompson of the 169th Regiment was a hero in the Civil War battle of Petersburg, Virginia.
23. *Troy Daily News*, 9 October 1873, p. 3.
24. *Utica Morning Herald*, 10 October 1873, p. 2.
25. Ibid., p. 2.
26. Baedeker, *The United* States, p. xxxi.
27. Reeve, 'Recollections of Wilkie Collins', pp. 460–1.
28. *Middleton (Connecticut) Daily Constitution*, 17 October 1873, p. 2.
29. *Syracuse Daily Courier*, 13 October 1873, p. 4.
30. *Albany Express* as quoted in the *Syracuse Daily Standard*, 9 October 1873, p. 4.
31. *Syracuse Daily Standard*, 13 October 1873, p. 4.
32. *Syracuse Journal*, 13 October 1873, p. 4.
33. *Syracuse Daily Courier*, 9 October, 1873, p. 4.
34. *Syracuse Journal*, 13 October 1873, p. 4.
35. *Public Ledger Almanac*, p. 38.
36. *Syracuse Daily Courier*, 13 October 1873, p. 4.
37. *Buffalo Express*, 15 October 1873, p, 1.
38. *Rochester Daily Union and Advertiser*, 11 October 1873, p. 1.
39. *Rochester Daily Union and Advertiser*, 13 October 1873, p. 2, and *Rochester Evening Express*, 13 October 1873, p. 3.
40. *Rochester Evening Express*, 14 October 1873, p. 2.
41. *Rochester Daily Union and Advertiser*, 14 October 1873, p. 2.
42. *Williamsport Gazette and Bulletin*, 13 October 1873, p. 1.
43. *New York Daily Graphic*, 16 October 1873, p. 3.
44. *Middleton (Connecticut) Daily Constitution*, 17 October 1873, p. 2.
45. *Dubuque (Iowa) Herald*, 22 October 1873.
46. *Dubuque (Iowa) Herald*, 28 October 1873.
47. *Buffalo Express*, 15 October 1873, p. 1.
48. *Men and Women: A Weekly Biographical and Social Journal*, 5 February 1887, p. 281.

5 Readings and Responses: Philadelphia, Boston and New York

1. *Philadelphia Press*, 16 October 1873, p. 5, and *Philadelphia Inquirer*, 16 October 1873, p. 5.
2. *Philadelphia Press*, 16 October 1873, p. 4.
3. *Philadelphia Inquirer*, 18 October 1873, p. 3.
4. *Philadelphia Press*, 18 October 1873, p. 2.
5. *Philadelphia Inquirer*, 18 October 1873, p. 3.

6. Ibid.
7. *Philadelphia Press*, 18 October 1873, p. 2.
8. Ibid., p. 2.
9. *Philadelphia Inquirer*, 18 October 1873, p. 3.
10. George W. Childs (1829–94) was a Philadelphia editor, journalist and philanthropist.
11. G. W. Childs, *Recollections* (Philadelphia, PA: Lippincott, 1892), p. 36.
12. *Public Face of Wilkie Collins*, vol. 2, p. 421.
13. Ibid., vol. 3, p. 87.
14. Ibid., vol. 2, p. 421.
15. *New York Tribune*, 23 October 1873, p. 5.
16. *New York Daily Graphic*, October 24 1873, p. 3.
17. A. Gasson, *Wilkie Collins: An Illustrated Guide* (Oxford: Oxford University Press, 1998), p. 138.
18. John Milton Hay (1838–1905) was an American statesman, diplomat, author and journalist, and was private secretary and assistant to Abraham Lincoln.
19. Col. William A. Seaver (d. 1883) was a well-known New York *raconteur* and writer of the 'Editor's Drawer' of *Harper's Magazine.* He became a close friend to Collins.
20. John Hay Collection, Brown University Library.
21. Oliver Wendell Holmes (1809–94) American physician and one of the best regarded poets of the nineteenth century.
22. See appendix for list of attendees.
23. *New York Tribune*, October 23 1873, p. 5.
24. *Boston Daily Evening Traveller*, 27 October 1873, p. 2.
25. *Boston Daily Evening Traveller*, 28 October 1873, p. 2.
26. *Boston Daily Evening Traveller*, 1 November 1873, p. 2.
27. *Public Face of Wilkie Collins*, vol. 3, p. 38.
28. Ibid., vol. 2, pp. 422–3.
29. *Boston Journal*, 30 October 1873.
30. Annie Fields, diary, 1 November 1873, Annie Fields papers, 1847–1912. Ms. N-1221. Massachusetts Historical Society.
31. Georgina Hogarth, Letter to Annie Fields, 30 August 1873, Huntington Library as quoted in Clarke, *Secret Life of Wilkie Collins*, pp. 144–5.
32. *King's Handbook of Boston*, 7th edn (Cambridge, MA: Moses King, 1885), p. 252.
33. *Boston Daily Evening Traveller*, 30 October 1873, p. 3.
34. Ibid., p. 2.
35. *Boston Daily Globe*, 31 October 1873, p. 5.
36. Ibid.
37. Ibid.
38. *Boston Evening Transcript*, 31 October 1873, p. 4.
39. *Boston Commonwealth*, 1 November 1873, p. 3.
40. *Boston Daily Evening Traveller*, 1 November 1873, p. 2.
41. Reeve, 'Recollections of Wilkie Collins', p. 461.
42. Sebastian Benson Schlesinger (1837–1917) moved to Boston from Hamburg in 1850 and by 1870 was acting German Consul and working at Naylor & Company, steel manufacturers. See *Public Face of Wilkie Collins*, vol. 2, p. 203.
43. Frank Ward (b. 1850) was the son of Wilkie's lifelong friend Charles James Ward (1814–33) who was an employee at Coutts & Co., a private bank in London. See *Public Face of Wilkie Collins*, vol. 1, p. 20.

44. S. Lonoff, 'Sex, Sense, and Nonsense: The Story of the Collins-Lear Friendship', in N. Smith and R. C. Terry (eds), *Wilkie Collins to the Forefront: Some Reassessments* (New York: AMS Press, 1995), pp. 37–51; pp. 46–7.
45. *Public Face of Wilkie Collins*, vol. 3, p. 4.
46. W. Collins, *The Haunted Hotel*, 2 vols (London: Chatto & Windus, 1878).
47. *Public Face of Wilkie Collins*, vol. 2, p. 422.
48. Ibid., vol. 2, p. 423.
49. Ibid., vol. 2, p. 426.
50. *Cleveland Daily Plain Dealer*, 9 January 1874, p. 3.
51. 'The Art of Not Posing – an Interview with Napoleon Sarony', *American Annual of Photography* (1896), p. 190.
52. Lonoff, 'Sex. Sense and Nonsense', p. 46.
53. W. Collins, *Heart and Science* (Peterborough, ON: Broadview, [1883] 1996), p. 36.
54. *Public Face of Wilkie Collins*, vol. 2, p. 422.
55. Ibid., vol. 2, p. 424.
56. *New York Times*, 11 November 1873, p. 8.
57. Globe Theater program for *The New Magdalen*, Friday, 9 May 1873 announcing the farewell engagement of Miss Carlotta Leclercq prior to her departure for Europe.
58. John Augustin Daly (1838–99) was the New York theatrical producer not only of *The New Magdalen* and *The Woman in White* during Collins's American tour, but also of *Man and Wife* three years earlier. He became friendly with Collins during their collaborations. See Clarke, *Secret Life of Wilkie Collins*, p. 182, for the story of how the manuscript of Collins's first unpublished novel, *Iolani* went from Daly's hands to eventual rediscovery and publication in 1999.
59. *New York Times*, 11 November 1873, p. 4.
60. Ibid.
61. *New York Daily Tribune*, 11 November 1873, p. 4.
62. *New York World*, 11 November 1873, p. 3
63. *New York Daily Tribune*, 11 November 1873, p. 4.
64. Ibid., p. 3
65. Ibid., p. 4
66. *New York Daily Graphic*, 11 November 1873, p. 2.
67. Ibid., p. 196.
68. *New York Daily Graphic*, 20 November 1873, p. 131.
69. R. P. Ashley, 'Wilkie Collins and the American Theater', *Nineteenth-Century Fiction*, 8 (March 1954), pp. 241–55; p. 250.
70. *Janesville (Wisconsin) Gazette*, 3 October 1873, and *Sedalia (Missouri) Democrat*, 15 November 1873.
71. *Reno (Nevada) State Journal*, 20 August 1874.
72. Peters, *King of Inventors*, p. 363.
73. Wilkie Collins, letter to Frederick Lehmann, 2 January 1874. Poetry Collection of the University Libraries, State University of New York at Buffalo.
74. *Public Face of Wilkie Collins*, vol. 2, p. 425.
75. *New York Daily Tribune*, 12 November 1873, p. 4.
76. *New York Daily Graphic*, 12 November 1873 p. 2.
77. *Public Face of Wilkie Collins*, vol. 2, p. 424.
78. *New York Times*, 12 November 1873, p. 5.
79. Ibid.

80. *New York Daily Graphic*, 12 November 1873, p. 2.
81. *New York Daily Tribune*, 12 November 1873, p. 4.
82. *New York Herald*, 12 November 1873, p. 6.
83. *Baltimore Sun*, 19 November, 1873, p. 4.
84. *Public Face of Wilkie Collins*, vol. 2, p. 425.
85. Ibid., vol. 2, p. 426.
86. Ibid., vol. 2, p. 426.
87. *Letters of Wilkie Collins*, vol. 2, p. 368.

6 The Second Swing: Baltimore and Washington

1. *Baltimorean*, 5 July 1873, p. 2.
2. J. T. Scharf, *History of Baltimore City and County* (Philadelphia, PA: Everts, 1881), p. 515.
3. Bryant, Stratton & Sadler's Business College, North Charles Street; at the time, considered one of the best business colleges in the United States. See ibid., p. 16.
4. *Baltimore Gazette*, 21 November 1873, p. 1.
5. John Elderkin, editor of the weekly New York *Fireside Companion*, which carried *The Dead Alive*. See *Public Face of Wilkie Collins*, vol. 2, p. 416.
6. *Baltimore Sun*, 29 November 1873, p. 4, and *Richmond Daily Dispatch*, 1 December 1873, p. 4.
7. John Hazlehurst Boneval Latrobe (1803–91) was a lawyer, inventor, public servant and father of seven-time Baltimore mayor, Ferdinand Claiborne Latrobe. See the *Dictionary of American Biography* (New York: Scribner's, 1943), pp. 27–8.
8. *Baltimore Gazette*, 27 November 1873, p. 1.
9. *Baltimore Sun*, 27 November 1873, p. 4.
10. *Baltimore Sun*, 29 November 1873, p. 1.
11. Ibid., p. 4.
12. Scharf, *History of Baltimore City and* County, p. 275.
13. *Public Face of Wilkie Collins*, vol. 3, p. 319.
14. *Baltimore Sun*, 29 November 1873, p. 4.
15. *Washington Evening Star*, 27 November 1873.
16. Possibly John Cessna, elected to the forty-third Congress in 1873 from the sixteenth district of Pennsylvania (which includes Tioga Country and which contains a town of Mill Creek and an area sometimes referred to as Mill Creek Bottom). See the *Biographical Directory of the United States Congress 1774–2005* (Washington DC: Government Printing Office, 2005).
17. A popular Washington restaurant of the time, located at Fifteenth St. and New York Avenue, catering to politicians and local celebrities.
18. Vinnie Ream (b. 1847), a noted writer and singer, was the first woman and the youngest artist to receive a US government commission for her statue of Lincoln in the Capitol Rotunda.
19. *Washington Capitol* and *Brooklyn Eagle*, 5 January 1874, p. 1, *Vermilionville (Louisiana) Lafayette Advertiser*, 7 February 1874, *Indiana (Pennsylvania) Progress*, 5 March 1874, *Portland (Oregon) Morning Oregonian*, 8 January 1874, etc.
20. *Public Face of Wilkie Collins*, vol. 3, p. 319.
21. *Washington Daily Critic*, 1 December 1873, p. 4.

7 A Change of Managers: The Northeast

1. *Public Face of Wilkie Collins*, vol. 2, p. 428.
2. Ibid., vol. 3, pp. 3–4.
3. Ibid., vol. 2, p. 429.
4. Ibid., vol. 2, p. 429.
5. *Boston Globe*, 1888, as quoted in C. Horner, *The Life of James Redpath* (New York: Barse & Hopkins, 1926), pp. 228–9.
6. *Providence Daily Journal*, 12 December 1873, p. 1.
7. Chalkey Collins, letter to his brother, 14 December 1873. RGS/173, Collins Family papers, Friends Historical Library, Swarthmore College.
8. Wilkie Collins, letter to Frederick Lehmann, 2 January 1874, Buffalo Historical Society. *Public Face of Wilkie Collins*, vol. 3, p. 3 has errors.
9. *Buffalo Daily Courier*, 8 October 1873, p. 1.
10. *Boston Commonwealth*, 13 December 1873, p. 2.
11. *Public Face of Wilkie Collins*, vol. 2, p. 422.
12. *Worcester Spy*, 14 November 1873, p. 2.
13. *New Bedford Republican Weekly Standard*, 27 November 1873, p. 4.
14. *Boston Daily Evening Traveller*, 15 December 1873, p. 2.
15. *Burlington (VT) Free Press*, 17 December 1873, p. 3.
16. *Hartford Daily Courant*, 20 December 1873, p. 1.
17. *Dubuque (Iowa) Herald*, 13 December 1873.
18. Ashley, 'Wilkie Collins and the American Theater', p. 252.
19. Reeve, 'Recollections of Wilkie Collins', p. 461.
20. Peters, *King of Inventors*, p. 363.
21. *New York Daily Graphic*, 12 December 1873, p. 302.
22. Wilkie Collins, letter to Jere Abbott, 17 December 1873, Lilly Library, Indiana University, Bloomington, Indiana.
23. *New Bedford Republican Standard*, 25 December 1873, p. 6.
24. Ibid.
25. Ibid.

8 The 'Double Difficulty': Montreal, Toronto and Buffalo

1. *Montreal Evening Star*, 22 December, p. 4
2. *Letters of Wilkie Collins*, vol. 2, p. 369.
3. *Montreal Gazette*, 22 December 1873, p. 2.
4. *Letters of Wilkie Collins*, vol. 2, p. 370.
5. *Montreal Gazette*, 22 December 1873, p. 2.
6. *Montreal Gazette*, 29 December 1873, p. 2.
7. *Montreal Herald* and *Daily Commercial Gazette*, 20 December 1873, p. 2.
8. *Montreal Gazette*, 22 December 1873, p. 1.
9. *Montreal Gazette* and *Montreal Herald*, 22 December 1873, p. 2.
10. *Montreal Evening Star*, 22 December 1873, p. 2.
11. Ibid.
12. *Montreal Gazette*, 23 December 1873, p. 2.
13. *Montreal Herald*, 23 December 1873, p. 1.
14. *Letters of Wilkie Collins*, vol. 2, p. 369.

15. *Toronto Daily Globe*, 24 December 1873, p. 4.
16. *Letters of Wilkie Collins*, vol. 2, p. 369.
17. Ibid., vol. 2, p. 371.
18. *Toronto Leader*, 27 December 1873.
19. *Letters of Wilkie Collins*, vol. 2, p. 371.
20. Ibid., vol. 2, p. 369.
21. Ibid., vol. 2, p. 371.
22. *Buffalo Daily Courier*, 27 December 1873, p. 2.
23. *Buffalo Daily Courier*, 3 January 1874, p. 1.
24. *Boston Commonwealth*, 20 January 1874, p. 2.
25. *Boston Commonwealth*, 31 January 1874, p. 2.
26. A. H. Laub, *The Buffalo Club, 1867–1967* (Buffalo, NY: The Club, 1968).
27. *Buffalo Commercial Advertiser*, 30 December 1873, p. 3.
28. *Buffalo Daily Courier*, 29 December 1873, p. 2.
29. *Buffalo Express*, 7 January 1874, p. 1.
30. Wilkie Collins, letter to Frederick Lehmann, 2 January 1874, The Poetry Collection of the University Libraries, State University of New York at Buffalo. Note that his letter appears in both R. C. Lehmann, *Memories of Half a Century* (London: Smith, Elder & Co., 1908) and in *Public Face of Wilkie Collins*, vol. 3, pp. 3–4, but with the two italicized lines omitted and various grammatical alterations that here have been restored as in the original letter.
31. Collins's pet name (meaning 'landlady') for Nina Chambers Lehmann, Fred's wife, whom he had known since before her marriage.
32. *Letters of Wilkie Collins*, vol. 2, pp. 369–1.
33. Ashley, 'Wilkie Collins and the American Theater', p. 244.
34. *Buffalo Daily Courier*, 3 January 1874, p. 2.
35. *Buffalo Express*, 3 January 1874, p. 1.
36. *Buffalo Commercial Advertiser*, 7 January 1874, p. 3

9 The Final Circuit: Cleveland, Detroit and Chicago

1. A review of five Erie, Pennsylvania newspapers for the period from 1 January 1874 through 22 January 1874 discloses no reference to Wilkie Collins. Accordingly, he apparently did not provide a reading there on his way from Buffalo to Cleveland, Ohio.
2. *Cleveland Daily Plain Dealer*, 3 January 1874, p. 3.
3. *Cleveland Reader*, 8 January 1874, p. 8 and *Cleveland Plain Dealer* 8 January 1874, p. 3.
4. *Cleveland Leader*, 9 January 1874, p. 7.
5. *Sandusky Daily Register*, 12 January 1874, p. 4.
6. *Sandusky Daily Register*, 5 January 1874, p. 4.
7. *Sandusky Daily Register*, 10 January 1874, p. 4.
8. *Public Face of Wilkie Collins*, vol. 3, p. 6.
9. *Toledo Blade*, 6 January 1874, p. 3.
10. *Toledo Blade*, 13 January 1874, p. 3.
11. *Detroit Free Press*, 6 January 1874, p. 3 and *Detroit Evening News*, 6 January 1874, p. 4.
12. Edward Askew Sothern (1826–81) was an English actor known for his comic roles.
13. *Detroit Evening News*, 15 January 1874, p. 4.
14. *Detroit Free Press*, 14 January 1874, p. 1.
15. *Landowner*, October 1873, p. 174.

16. *Chicago Times*, 17 January 1874, p. 10.
17. *Chicago Times*, 12 October 1873.
18. *Chicago Times*, 24 October 1873.
19. *Chicago Tribune*, 17 January 1874, p. 5. The City Sealer was the person duly authorized to enforce and administer the weights and measures program.
20. *Landowner*, October 1873, p. 174.
21. *Chicago Tribune*, 17 January 1874, p. 5.
22. *Chicago Evening Journal*, 17 January 1874, p. 6.
23. *Public Face of Wilkie Collins*, vol. 3, p. 4.
24. *Boston Evening Transcript*, 22 January 1874, p. 4.
25. In a letter to his cousin, Alexander Gray, dated 26 May 1888, Collins apologized for not visiting him on his American tour. See D. C. Whitton, *The Grays of Salisbury* (San Francisco, CA: Whitton, 1976), p. 23, and *Letters of Wilkie Collins*, vol. 2, p. 558.
26. *Public Face of Wilkie Collins*, vol. 3, p. 5.
27. Ibid., vol. 3, p. 7.
28. Ibid., vol. 3, p. 9.
29. The Great Chicago Fire started on 8 October 1871 and burned for thirty-six hours, destroying three and a half square miles in the heart of the city. It levelled more than 18,000 structures, leaving 100,000 residents homeless and killing more than 300. Aided by an outpouring of charity from around the world, Chicagoans brought about a remarkable reconstruction. James Grossman (ed.), *The Encyclopedia of Chicago* (Chicago, IL: University of Chicago Press, 2004), p. 297.
30. *Public Face of Wilkie Collins*, vol. 3, p. 8.
31. Five pounds in 1871 would be roughly equal to 310 pounds in 2005. See www.measuringworth.com (accessed 18 January 2008).
32. Wilkie Collins, letter to Committee of the American Chicago Relief Fund, 31 October 1871, Susan Hanes.
33. *Public Face of Wilkie Collins*, vol. 3, p. 10.

10 Arguments and Accolades: Return to New England

1. *Detroit Evening News*, 20 January 1874, p. 4.
2. *Dickens on America and the Americans*, ed. M. Slater (Austin: University of Texas, 1978), p. 222.
3. *Letters of Wilkie Collins*, vol. 2, p. 375.
4. *Public Face of Wilkie Collins*, vol. 3, p. 12.
5. *Salem Register*, 29 January, 1874, p. 2.
6. *Salem Post*, 4 February 1874, p. 2.
7. *Boston Daily Evening Traveller*, 27 January 1874, p. 3.
8. *Boston Daily Evening Traveller*, 2 February 1874, p. 1.
9. *Public Face of Wilkie Collins*, vol. 3, p. 15.
10. *Dickens: Public Readings*, p. 32.
11. *Public Face of Wilkie Collins*, vol. 3, p. 13.
12. *Springfield Republican*, 6 February 1874, p. 6.
13. *Worcester Daily Spy*, 4 February 1874, p. 3.
14. Built in 1857 by the Worcester County Mechanics Association, the Mechanics Hall was one of the nation's finest pre-Civil War concert halls. The Hall was completely restored

in 1977 and in 2006 is still a unique home to the performing arts. See www.mechanicshall.org (accessed 18 January 2008).

15. *Worcester Evening Gazette*, 7 February 1874, p. 2.
16. *Worcester Daily Press*, 7 February 1874, p. 2.
17. *Worcester Evening Gazette*, 7 February 1874, p. 2.
18. *Public Face of Wilkie Collins*, vol. 3, p. 15.
19. *Boston Evening Transcript*, 2 March 1874, p. 1.
20. The unfortunate Rev. Mr Parry had encountered a series of regrettable events before the Wilkie Collins-American Literary Bureau debacle. Manager of the Anglo-American Lecture Course in Worcester, he was responsible for the cancellation of a Ghost Lecture by Professor John Henry Pepper of London scheduled for Friday, 3 October 1873 due to the late arrival of apparatus necessary for the entertainment. In a letter to the public appearing in the 4 October issue of the *Spy*, Rev. Parry defended his decision, saying that the entertainment would have been a failure, and promised to refund money if requested. He referred to Mr Williams, the manager of the Massachusetts office of the American Literary Bureau, who 'worked, with me, like a horse to make the lecture a success'. Prof. Pepper retorted in the paper that he would go on with his program, proving that it was not a fiasco, and would expect to be paid for his performance. If he was not paid, he would open the doors for free to anyone who paid for tickets. It was further reported in the 4 November edition of the *Spy* that Rev. Parry was asked to resign as pastor of the Old South Church because some members of the congregation did not like the way he illustrated his sermons. According to a file at the American Antiquarian Society, William M. Parry became minister of Tabernacle Congregational Church of Worcester in 1874 and remained there until his death in 1879.
21. The italicized line is quoted in Collins's letter to Redpath, 10 February 1874. See *Public Face of Wilkie Collins*, vol. 3, p. 15.
22. *Worcester Evening Gazette*, 9 February 1874, p. 2, and *Worcester Spy*, 9 February 1874, p. 1.
23. *Public Face of Wilkie Collins*, vol. 3, p. 15.
24. Ibid.
25. *Boston Evening Transcript*, 17 February 1874, p. 1.
26. Menu, PM1 Collins, W. Pierpont Morgan Library.
27. *Boston Evening Transcript*, 17 February 1874, p. 1.
28. *Boston Daily Globe*, 17 February 1874, p. 1.
29. Menu, PM1 Collins, W. Pierpont Morgan Library.
30. *Boston Evening Standard*, 17 February 1874, p. 1.
31. *Boston Daily Evening Traveller*, 17 February 1874, p. 1.
32. *Public Face of Wilkie Collins*, vol. 3, p. 16.

11 Winding Down: New York and Wallingford

1. *Public Face of Wilkie Collins*, vol. 3, p. 16.
2. Ibid., vol. 3, pp. 16–17.
3. Ibid., vol. 3, p. 16.
4. *Letters of Henry Wordsworth Longfellow*, ed. A. Hilen (Cambridge, MA: Belknap, 1982), p. 723, n. 724.
5. *Boston Daily Evening Traveller*, 28 February 1874, p. 1.
6. *Boston Daily Evening Traveller*, 27 February 1874, p. 3.

7. *Boston Daily Globe*, 28 February 1874, p. 4.
8. *Boston Evening Transcript*, 27 February 1874, p. 4.
9. S. Wilson, *The Omni Parker House: A Brief History of America's Longest Continuously Operating Hotel* (Boston, MA: Omni Parker House, 2001), p. 24.
10. *Daily Graphic*, 2 March, 1874, p. 1.
11. *Public Face of Wilkie Collins*, vol. 3, p. 18.
12. Ibid., vol. 3, p. 17.
13. *Letters of Wilkie Collins*, vol. 3, p. 381.
14. *Fort Wayne (Indiana) Daily Sentinel*, 28 March 1874.
15. *Public Face of Wilkie Collins*, vol. 3, p. 320, n. 7.
16. *New York Times*, 2 March 1874, p. 8.
17. Collins, 'Recollections of Charles Fechter', p. 172.
18. *Hartford Daily Courant*, 5 March 1874, p. 2.
19. *Oneida Circular*, 16 March 1874, p. 92.
20. G. W. Noyes, *Free Love in Utopia: John Humphrey Noyes and the Origin of the Oneida Community* (Urbana: University of Illinois Press, 2001), p. 9
21. *Oneida Circular*, 16 March 1874, p. 92. See also C. Nordhoff, *The Communistic Societies of the United States* (New York: Harper & Bros., 1875), pp. 259–76, which was a part of Collins's library at the time of his death. See also W. Baker, *Wilkie Collins's Library: A Reconstruction* (Westport, CT: Greenwood Press, 2002), p. 136.
22. *New Haven Register*, 5 March 1874, p. 3.
23. Ibid., p. 3.
24. *Oneida Circular*, 16 March 1874, p. 92.
25. Charles S. Joslyn (1832–1906) joined the Oneida Association on 12 May 1849 at the age of sixteen. Prior to attending college, Joslyn worked at the Community as a farmer, printer, music teacher and painter. One of twelve young men sent to Yale by the Community, he received his degree in three years and in 1867 was admitted to the bar after attending law school at Columbia University. Thereafter he functioned as an attorney for the Community as well as a music teacher. He fathered one Community child with Harriet Allen in 1859, whom he subsequently married after the breakup of the Community in 1879. See J. Teeple, *The Oneida Family: Genealogy of a 19th Century Perfectionist Commune* (Oneida, NY: Oneida Community Historical Committee, 1985), pp. 48–9.
26. *New Haven Register*, 5 March 1874, p. 3.
27. Oneida Creek was a small river in New York between Madison and Oneida counties, near the location of the main Oneida Community.
28. Agapemone was an English religious community of men and women, holding all goods in common. It was founded (*c.* 1850) at the village of Spaxton, Somerset, by Henry James Prince (1811–99), Samuel Starky, and others. Prince and Starky were clergymen who had left (*c.* 1843) the Church of England after Prince claimed that the Holy Ghost had taken up residence in his body. The Agapemonites proclaimed the imminent second coming of Jesus.
29. *Oneida Circular*, 16 March 1874, p. 92.
30. W. Collins, *The Fallen Leaves* (Coln St. Aldwyns, Gloucester: Echo, [1879] 2005), pp. 23–4.
31. Baker, *Wilkie Collins's Library*, p. 136.
32. Wilkie Collins, letter to C. S. Joslyn, 3 April 1879. Oneida Collection, Special Collections Research Center, Syracuse University.
33. *Public Face of Wilkie Collins*, vol. 3, p. 19.

34. Ibid., vol. 3, p. 18.
35. Ibid., vol. 3, p. 21.
36. *Letters of Wilkie Collins*, vol. 2, p. 382.
37. Ibid., vol. 2, p. 396.

Conclusion: Wilkie Collins and the American People

1. *Public Face of Wilkie Collins*, vol. 2, p. 420.
2. *Albany Evening Journal*, 8 October 1893.
3. Mary Bradford, letter to her sister, 5 June 1874. Lynn Historical Museum, Lynn, MA.
4. Robinson, *Wilkie Collins: A Biography*, p. 273.
5. Peters, *King of Inventors*, pp. 365–6.
6. *New York Daily Graphic*, 29 September 1873, p. 2.
7. *New York Daily Graphic*, 6 October 1873, p. 2.
8. *New York Daily Graphic*, 10 October 1873, p. 3.
9. *New York Daily Graphic* 15 October 1873, p. 2.
10. *New York Daily Graphic*, 11 October 1873, p. 3.
11. *Fort Wayne (Indiana) Weekly Sentinel*, 10 December 1873.
12. *Indiana (Pennsylvania) Progress*, 4 September 1873.
13. *Detroit Evening News*, 22 January, 1874, p. 3.
14. *Cleveland Reader*, 30 September 1873, p. 2.
15. *The Golden Age*, as quoted in *Detroit Free Press*, 18 January 1874, vol. 1, p. 1.
16. *Decatur (Illinois) Republican*, 15 January 1874.
17. *Rochester (New York) Union and Advertiser*, 10 October 1873, p. 2.
18. *New York Daily Graphic*, 22 October 1873, p. 6.
19. *New York Herald*, 27 September 1873, p. 10.
20. *Dubuque (Iowa) Herald*, 22 October 1873.
21. *Montreal Gazette*, 19 December 1873, p. 3.
22. *Boston Commonwealth*, 1 November 1873, p. 3.
23. *Chicago Inter-Ocean*, 17 January 1874, p. 2.
24. *Boston Commonwealth*, 1 November 1873, p. 3.
25. *Sandusky Daily Register*, 10 January 1874, p. 4.
26. *Chicago Tribune*, 17 January 1874, p. 5.
27. *Toledo Blade*, 13 January 1874, p. 3.
28. *Cleveland Reader*, 8 January 1874, p. 8.
29. *Syracuse Daily Courier*, 13 October 1873, p. 4.
30. *Public Face of Wilkie Collins*, vol. 4, p. 21.
31. Gasson, *Wilkie Collins: An Illustrated Guide*, p. 82
32. Gill published *The Frozen Deep* and *Alicia Warlock (a Mystery) and Other Stories* in 1875.
33. *Letters of Wilkie Collins*, vol. 2, p. 382.

Appendix E: Press Portraits

1. *Rochester Union and Advertiser*, 10 October 1873, p. 2.
2. *Syracuse Daily Journal*, 8 October 1873, p. 4.
3. *Buffalo Commercial Advertiser*, 7 October 1873, p. 3.
4. *Boston Commonwealth*, 8 November 1873, p. 4.

5. *Toledo Blade*, 13 January 1874, p. 3.
6. *Chicago Tribune*, 17 January 1874, p. 5.
7. *Buffalo Express*, 7 January 1874, p. 1.
8. *Albany Evening Journal*, 8 October 1873, p. 3.
9. *New York Daily Graphic*, 12 November 1873, p. 2.
10. *Springfield Republican*, 6 February 1874, p. 6.
11. *Montreal Gazette*, 19 December 1873, p. 3.
12. *Chicago Inter-Ocean*, 17 January 1874, p. 2.
13. *Cleveland Daily Plain Dealer*, 9 January 1874, p. 3.
14. *Syracuse Daily Journal*, 8 October 1873, p. 4.
15. *Boston Commonwealth*, 8 November 1873, p. 4.
16. *Buffalo Express*, 7 January 1874, p. 1.
17. *Albany Evening Journal*, 8 October 1873, p. 3.
18. *New York Herald*, 27 September 1873, p. 10.
19. *New York Daily Graphic*, 22 October 1873, p. 6.
20. *Syracuse Daily Courier*, 13 October 1873, p. 4.
21. *New York Daily Graphic*, 12 November 1873, p. 2.
22. *Dubuque (Iowa) Herald*, 22 October 1873.
23. *Montreal Gazette*, 19 December 1873, p. 3.
24. *Boston Commonwealth*, 1 November 1873, p. 3.
25. *Chicago Inter-Ocean*, 17 January 1874, p. 2.
26. *Chicago Tribune*, 17 January 1874, p. 5.
27. *Dubuque (Iowa) Herald*, 4 October 1873, p. 3.
28. *Albany Evening Journal*, 8 October 1873, p. 3.
29. *Syracuse Daily Courier*, 13 October 1873, p. 4.
30. *Utica Morning Herald*, 10 October 1873, p. 2.
31. *Cleveland Leader*, 9 January 1874, p. 7.
32. *Albany Argus*, 8 October 1873, p. 4.
33. *Boston Commonwealth*, 1 November 1873, p. 3.
34. *Toledo Blade*, 13 January 1874, p. 3.
35. *Chicago Inter-Ocean*, 17 January 1874, p. 1.
36. *Chicago Evening Journal*, 17 January 1874, p. 6.
37. *Philadelphia Inquirer*, 18 October 1873, p. 3.
38. *Utica Morning Herald*, 10 October 1873, p. 2.
39. *Sandusky Daily Register*, 10 January 1874, p. 4.
40. *Cleveland Reader*, 8 January 1874, p. 8.
41. *Chicago Tribune*, 17 January 1874, p. 5.
42. *Detroit Evening News*, 14 January 1874, p. 4.
43. *Albany Argus*, 8 October 1873, p. 4.
44. *Philadelphia Press*, 18 October 1873, p. 2.
45. *New York Daily Graphic*, 20 October 1873, p. 3.
46. *Syracuse Daily Courier*, 13 October 1873, p. 4.

WORKS CITED

Libraries and Archives

Canada
- *Montreal, QC*
  - Grande Bibliothèque du Quebec
  - McGill University Libraries
    - McLennan Library
- *Ottawa, ON*
  - Library and Archives Canada
- *Niagara Falls, ON*
  - Niagara Falls Public Library
- *Toronto, ON*
  - Toronto Reference Library

Connecticut
- *Hartford*
  - Connecticut State Library
    - History and Genealogy Unit
- *New Haven*
  - New Haven Public Library
  - Yale University Libraries
    - Beinecke Rare Book and Manuscript Library
- *Wallingford*
  - Wallingford Historical Society
  - Wallingford Public Library

District of Columbia
- *Washington DC*
  - Folger Shakespeare Library
    - Manuscripts Division
  - Historical Society of Washington, DC
  - Library of Congress
    - Rare Book and Special Collections Division
      - Manuscript Division

Delaware
- *Winterthur*
  - Winterthur Museum

Illinois
- *Chicago*
  - Chicago History Museum
    - Research Library
  - Harold Washington Library Center
    - Special Collections and Preservation Department
  - Newberry Library
  - University of Chicago Library
    - Special Collections Research Center

Massachusetts
- *Amherst*
  - Amherst College
    - Robert Frost Library
      - Department of Archives and Special Collections
- *Boston*
  - Boston Athenaeum
    - Special Collections
  - Boston Public Library
    - Rare Books and Manuscripts
  - Massachusetts Historical Society
    - Research Library
- *Cambridge*
  - Harvard University Libraries
    - Houghton Library
- *Lynn*
  - Lynn Museum and Historical Society
    - Research Library
- *New Bedford*
  - Free Library of New Bedford
  - Whaling Museum Research Library
- *Northampton*
  - Smith College Library
    - Mortimer Rare Book Room
- *Salem*
  - Peabody Essex Museum
    - Phillips Library
- *Williamstown*
  - Williams College Libraries
    - Chapin Library of Rare Books
- *Worcester*
  - American Antiquarian Society
  - Worcester Historical Museum
    - Research Library
  - Worcester Public Library

Maryland
Baltimore
Enoch Pratt Free Library
Special Collections Department
Maryland Historical Society
Research Library

Maine
Portland
Maine Historical Society
Research Library

Michigan
Ann Arbor
University of Michigan Libraries
University Library
William L. Clements Library
Detroit
Detroit Public Library
Burton Historical Collection

New Jersey
Princeton
Princeton University Library
Department of Rare Books and Special Collections

New York
Albany
New York State Archives
New York State Library
Buffalo
Buffalo & Erie County Historical Society
Research Library
Buffalo & Erie County Public Library
State University of New York at Buffalo
The Poetry Collection of the University Libraries
Highland Falls
Highland Falls Library
Town of Highlands Historical Society
New York
Brooklyn Public Library
Columbia University Libraries
Butler Library, Rare Book and Manuscripts Division
Morgan Library and Museum
New York Public Library
Berg Collection of English and American Literature
Manuscripts and Archives Division
Niagara Falls
Niagara Falls Public Library

Rochester
Central Library of Rochester and Monroe County, NY
University of Rochester
Rush Rhees Library
Rochester Historical Society
Syracuse
Onondaga County Central Library
Local History and Genealogy Department
Syracuse University Library
Special Collections Research Center
Troy
Rensselaer County Historical Research Library
Troy Public Library
Local History Collections

Ohio
Cleveland
Cleveland Public Library
Cleveland State University Library
Special Collections
Western Reserve Historical Society
Library and Archives
Sandusky
Sandusky Library
Archives Research Center
Toledo
Toledo Public Library

Pennsylvania
Doylestown
Bucks County Historical Society
Erie
Erie Public Library
Philadelphia
Historical Society of Pennsylvania
Free Library of Pennsylvania
Manuscripts and Special Collections
University of Pennsylvania Library
Rare Books and Manuscripts
Swarthmore
Swarthmore College
Friends Historical Library

Rhode Island
Newport
Redwood Library
Providence
Brown University Libraries
John Hay Library

Rhode Island Historical Society
Research Library
Rhode Island State Library

Virginia
Charlottesville
University of Virginia Libraries
Small Special Collections Library

Vermont
Burlington
Burlington Public Library
University of Vermont Library

Wisconsin
Madison
State Historical Society of Wisconsin
Archives Division

Manuscript Sources

Bigelow, John. Journal. John Bigelow Papers, Manuscripts and Archives Division, New York Public Library, Astor, Lenox and Tilden Foundations.

Bradford, Mary. Letters from England, 1874. Lynn Museum, Lynn Massachusetts.

Collins, Chalkey. Letter to his brother, 14 December 1873. RGS/173 Collins Family Papers. Friends Historical Library of Swarthmore College.

Collins, Wilkie. Letter to Frederick Lehmann, 2 January 1874. Poetry Collection of the University Libraries, State University of New York at Buffalo.

—, Letter to Committee of the American Chicago Relief Fund. 31 Oct. 1871. Susan Hanes

—, Letter to C. S. Joslyn. 3 April. 1879. Oneida Collection, Special Collections Research Center, Syracuse University.

—, Letter to Jere Abbott. 17 Dec. 1873. Lily Library Special Collections. Indiana University, Bloomington.

—, Letter to Joseph J. Casey, 12 July 1873. Simon Gratz Collection (ex. American Poets), Historical Society of Pennsylvania.

Fields, Annie. Diary. Annie Fields papers, 1847–1912. Ms. N-1221. Massachusetts Historical Society.

Parton, John, letter to Ellen, 10 January 1874, Family papers, bMS Am 1248.4, Houghton Library, Harvard College Library.

Periodicals

Albany Argus.

Albany Evening Journal.

Albany Express.

Appleton's Journal.

Atlanta Constitution.

Baltimore Gazette.

Baltimore Sun.

Baltimorean.

Boston Commonwealth.

Boston Daily Evening Traveller.

Boston Daily Globe.

Boston Evening Standard.

Boston Evening Transcript.

Brooklyn Eagle.

Buffalo Commercial Advertiser.

Buffalo Daily Courier.

Buffalo Express.

Burlington (VT) Free Press.

Chicago Evening Journal.

Chicago Inter-Ocean.

Chicago Times.

Chicago Tribune.

Cleveland Daily Plain Dealer.

Cleveland Leader.

Cleveland Reader.

Commercial Advertiser.

Daily Commercial Gazette.

Daily Graphic.

Decatur (Illinois) Republican.

Detroit Evening News.

Detroit Free Press.

Dubuque (Iowa) Herald.

Edwardsville (Illinois) Intelligencer.

Fort Wayne (Indiana) Gazette.

Frank Leslie's Illustrated Newspaper.

Frank Leslie's Illustrated Newspaper Supplement.

Harper's Weekly.

Hartford Daily Courant.

Indiana (Pennsylvania) Progress.

Janesville (Wisconsin) Gazette.

Kingston (Ontario) Whig.

Lafayette (Louisiana) Advertiser.

Landowner.

Men and Women: A Weekly Biographical and Social Journal.

Middleton (Connecticut) Daily Constitution.

Montreal Evening Star.

Montreal Gazette.

Montreal Herald.

New Bedford Republican Standard.

New Bedford Republican Weekly Standard.

New Haven Register.

New York Daily Graphic.

New York Daily Tribune.

New York Herald.

New York Journal.

New York Sunday Mercury.

New York Times.

New York Tribune.

New York World.

News of the Highlands.

Oneida Circular.

Philadelphia Inquirer.

Philadelphia Press.

Portland (Oregon) Morning Oregonian.

Providence Daily Journal.

Reno (Nevada) State Journal.

Richmond Daily Dispatch.

Rochester Daily Union and Advertiser.

Rochester Evening Express.

Rochester (New York) Union and Advertiser.

Salem Post.

Salem Register.

Sandusky Daily Register.

Springfield Republican.

Syracuse Daily Courier.

Syracuse Daily Standard.

Syracuse Journal.

Toledo Blade.

Toronto Daily Globe.

Toronto Leader.

Troy Daily Press.

Troy Daily Times.

Utica Morning Herald.

Vermilionville (Louisiana) Lafayette Advertiser.

Washington Capitol and Brooklyn Eagle.

Washington Evening Star.

Williamsport Gazette and Bulletin.

Worcester Daily Press.

Worcester Evening Gazette.

Worcester Spy.

Primary Sources

American Annual of Photography (1896).

Archer, F., *An Actor's Notebooks* (London: Paul, 1912).

Baedaker, K., *The United States, with an Excursion into Mexico: Handbook for Travellers*, 1st edn (Leipsic: Baedeker, 1893).

Bigelow, J., *Retrospections of an Active Life* 5 vols (Garden City, NY: Doubleday, 1913).

Bryant, W. C., *The Letters of William Cullen Bryant*, ed. W. C. Bryant II and T. Voss (New York: Fordham University Press, 1992).

Century Club. Menu for Banquet to Wilkie Collins, 1 October 1873. Wilkie Collins, Morgan Library.

Childs, G. W., *Recollections* (Philadelphia, PA: Lippincott, 1892).

Collins, W., *The Haunted Hotel*, 2 vols (London: Chatto & Windus, 1878).

—, *The Fallen Leaves* (Coln St. Aldwyns, Gloucester: Echo, [1879] 2005).

—, 'Wilkie Collins's Recollections of Charles Fechter', in K. Field, *Charles Albert Fechter* (New York: Blom, [1882], 1969), pp. 154–73.

—, *Heart and* Science, ed. S. Farmer (Peterborough, ON: Broadview, [1883] 1996).

—, *The Letters of Wilkie Collins*, ed. W. Baker and W. M. Clarke, 2 vols (Houndmills: Macmillan, 1999).

—, *The Public Face of Wilkie Collins: The Collected* Letters, ed. W. Baker, A. Gasson, G. Law, and P. Lewis, 4 vols (London: Pickering & Chatto, 2005).

Crowe, E., *With Thackeray in America* (London: Cassell and Company, 1893).

Curtis, G. W., *Literary and Social Essays* (New York: Harper & Brothers, 1894).

Dickens, C., *Charles Dickens: The Public Readings*, ed. P. Collins (Oxford: Clarendon Press, 1975).

—, *Dickens on America and the Americans*, ed. M. Slater (Austin: University of Texas Press, 1978).

Dickens C., and W. Collins, *The Letters of Charles Dickens and Wilkie Collins*, ed. L. Hutton (New York: Harper & Bros., 1892).

Dolby, G., *Charles Dickens as I Knew Him* (London: T. Fisher Unwin, 1885).

Elderkin, J., *A Brief History of the Lotos Club* (New York: The Club, 1895).

Fitzgerald, P., *Memoirs of an Author*, 2 vols (London: R. Bentley and Son, 1894).

Globe Theater, Boston. Printed Programme, *The New Magdalen*. 9 May 1873. Susan Hanes.

Harper, J. H., *The House of Harper: A Century of Publishing in Franklin Square* (New York: Harper, 1912).

Horner, C. F., *The Life of James Redpath* (New York: Barse & Hopkins, 1926).

King's Handbook of Boston, 7th edn (Cambridge, MA: Moses King, 1885).

Laub, A. H., *The Buffalo Club, 1867–1967* (Buffalo, NY: The Club, 1968).

Longfellow, H. W., *Letters of Henry Wordsworth Longfellow*, ed. A. Hilen (Cambridge, MA: Belknap, 1982).

Lotos Club. Invitation to Dinner, 27 September 1873. Wilkie Collins, New York Public Library Special Collections.

Mercer, W. R., 'Notes on the Life of Charles Albert Fechter', in *A Collection of Papers Read Before the Bucks County Historical Society*. 4 vols (Bucks Co., PA: The Bucks County Historical Society, 1917), pp. 504–10.

Nordhoff, C., *The Communistic Societies of the United States: From Personal Visit and Observation* (New York: Harper & Bros., 1875).

Norton, C. E., 'Charles Dickens', *North American Review*, 106 (April 1868), pp. 671–2.

Public Ledger Almanac (Philadelphia, PA: Childs, 1874).

Reed, T. (ed.), *Modern Eloquence: After-Dinner Speeches A-D* (Philadelphia, PA: John Morris, 1900).

Reeve, W., 'Recollections of Wilkie Collins', *Chambers's Journal*, 9 (December 1905–November 1906), pp. 458–61.

Walford, L. B., *Memories of Victorian London* (London: Arnold, 1912).

Secondary Sources

Ashley, R. P., 'Wilkie Collins and the American Theater', *Nineteenth-Century Fiction*, 8 (March 1954), pp. 241–55.

Bachman, M. K., and D. R. Cox (eds), *Reality's Dark Light: The Sensational Wilkie Collins* (Knoxville: University of Tennessee Press, 2003).

Baker, W., *Wilkie Collins's Library: A Reconstruction* (Westport, CT: Greenwood, 2002).

Biographical Directory of the United States Congress 1774–2005 (Washington DC: Government Printing Office, 2005).

Clarke, W., *The Secret Life of Wilkie Collins*, 2nd edn (Thrupp, Gloucester: Sutton, 2004).

Davis, N. P., *The Life of Wilkie Collins* (Urbana: University of Illinois Press, 1956).

Dictionary of American Biography (New York: Scribner's, 1943).

Fisher, J. L. (ed.), *Lives of Victorian Literary Figures V, Vol. 3: William Thackeray* (London: Pickering & Chatto, 2007).

Garraty, J. and M. C. Carnes (eds), *American National Biography*, 24 vols (New York: Oxford University Press, 1999).

Gasson, A., *Wilkie Collins: An Illustrated Guide* (Oxford: Oxford University Press, 1998).

Grossman, J. (ed.), *The Encyclopedia of Chicago* (Chicago, IL: University of Chicago, 2004).

Hyder, C. K., 'Wilkie Collins in America', *Studies in English in Honour of Raphael Dorman O'Leary and Seldon Lincoln Whitcomb* (Lawrence: University of Kansas, 1940), pp. 50–8.

Laub, A. H., *The Buffalo Club, 1867–1967* (Buffalo, NY: The Club, 1968).

Lonoff, S., 'Sex, Sense, and Nonsense: The Story of the Collins-Lear Friendship', in N. Smith and R. C. Terry (eds), *Wilkie Collins to the Forefront: Some Reassessments* (New York: AMS Press, 1995), pp. 37–51.

Nayder, L., *Wilkie Collins* (New York: Twayne, 1997).

Noyes, G. W., *Free Love in Utopia: John Humphrey Noyes and the Origin of the Oneida Community* (Urbana: University of Illinois Press, 2001).

Peters, C. *The King of Inventors: A Life of Wilkie Collins* (Princeton, NJ: Princeton University Press, 1991).

Pykett, L., *Wilkie Collins* (Oxford: Oxford: University Press, 2005).

Ray, A. G., *The Lyceum and Public Culture in the Nineteenth-Century United States* (East Lansing: Michigan State Univesity Press, 2005).

Robinson, K., *Wilkie Collins: A Biography* (London: Bodley Head, 1951).

Scharf, J. T., *History of Baltimore City and County* (Philadelphia, PA: Everts, 1881).

Taylor, J. B. (ed.), *The Cambridge Companion to Wilkie Collins* (New York: Cambridge University Press, 2006).

Teeple, J., *The Oneida Family: Genealogy of a 19th Century Perfectionist Commune* (Oneida, NY: Oneida Community Historical Committee, 1985).

Whitton, D. C., *The Grays of Salisbury* (San Francisco, CA: Whitton, 1976).

Wilson, S., *The Omni Parker House: A Brief History of America's Longest Continuously Operating Hotel* (Boston, MA: Omni Parker House, 2001).

Zinn, H., *A People's History of the United States* (New York: HarperCollins, 2003).

INDEX